RICHARD ROBINSON OF COUNTERSETT 1628 – 1693

AND

THE QUAKERS OF WENSLEYDALE

by
DAVID S. HALL

William Sessions Limited,
York, England

ISBN 1 85072 048 7

© David S. Hall, 1989

Published 1989

Printed in 10/11 point Times Typeface
by William Sessions Limited
The Ebor Press
York, England

Contents

		page
	Illustrations	vi
	The Robinson Family Genealogy	viii
	Acknowledgements	x
	Foreword by Dr. Arthur Raistrick	xi
	Introduction	xii
PART I	**The First Quaker in Wensleydale**	
	The Man Convinced	1
	Continuing Faith	6
	Sufferings and other Exercises	11
PART II	**Later Generations**	
	Faith and Prosperity	20
	The Last of the Yeomen	29
	Conviction Fades and is Lost	36
PART III	**Stones and Mortar**	
	Countersett Hall	42
	Semerdale Hall	48
	Holly House, Boar Inn, Verity House and Coopermire	53
PART IV	**One Meeting House for all**	
	Bainbridge Friends Meeting House	58
	Hawes Friends Meeting House	61
	Countersett Friends Meeting House	64
	Countersett School	69
	Abbreviations	73
	Notes and References	74
	Index	85

Illustrations

	Page
Richard Robinson's personal seal drawn from an original impression surviving in the Philip Swale manuscripts. Pen and ink drawing by DSH, 1974.	ii
Countersett Hall as it was in Richard Robinson's time with three mullioned windows restored from surviving evidence. Pen and ink drawing by DSH, 1967.	xvi
Countersett Hall date stone showing the initials of Richard and Margaret Robinson and the date 1650. Pen and ink drawing by DSH, 1967.	1
Countersett from an old postcard showing the Hall with pointing fresh from the alterations of 1885. Note the tall chimney on Elsie House, the White House coloured white and the Board Inn (also white) with its signboard prominently displayed. Photograph by J. B. Smithson, Leyburn.	3
Title page from *A Blast blown out of the North* which Richard Robinson wrote in prison at Richmond and had published in 1680. From the copy in North Yorkshire County Library, Northallerton.	12
Richard Robinson's letter to Philip Swale concerning his visit to Bolton Hall to explain 'our princeples' to the Marquess of Winchester. From Countersett, 29 November, 1683. NYCRO, R/Q/R 5/90.	15
Rachel Robinson's receipt for Philip Swale's legacy, 16 March, 1687 [o.s.], Semerdale Deeds.	17
Michael Robinson's letter to John Chaytor of Richmond, as a trustee of Philip Swale's estate, concerning new trials at the lead mines in Swaledale. From Countersett, 4 November, 1688. NYCRO, R/Q/R 5/232.	21
Countersett Friends Meeting House as completed in 1778 with the courtyard of 1781. Photograph by E. Lingford of Darlington and published in J. W. Steel: *Early Friends in the North*, 1905. Reproduced by permission of the Library Committee of London Yearly Meeting of the Religious Society of Friends.	23
The old wooden staircase at Countersett Hall with stout turned balusters under a strong banister rail. The staircase, pine panelling and hams have now gone. Photograph by A. J. Heal of Leeds, 1952.	26
The letter John Robinson wrote about his 'difference' with James Metcalfe over a right of way and the repair of drystone walls, 6 November, 1717. NYCRO, R/Q/R 16/30.	27
Holly House date stone showing Joshua Robinson's initials and the date 1740. Pen and ink drawing by DSH, 1979.	31
Semerwater bridge as built by Quaker initiative about 1770 and restored by the North Riding Quarter Sessions in 1874. Photograph by DSH, 1967.	34

	Page
Plan of the Upper House area of Bowling, Bradford, the home of the Robinson family from 1778 to 1811. Ordnance Survey map, 1:1056 of Bradford, sheet 12, surveyed in 1848, published 1852. Bradford Libraries and Information Service.	37
Countersett Hall's kitchen range with massive stone jambs, lintel and moulded mantelpiece, set between 18th century cupboards and panelling. The cast iron range (oven, side boiler, sooker stone and reckon) was taken out in 1957. Pen and ink drawing, from memory, by DSH, 1966.	43
Plan of Countersett Hall showing the pre-17th century dwelling (with salt box and brick lined bread oven), to which Richard and Margaret Robinson came in 1650. Also their new parlour and porch. The later accommodation, called Elsie House, was occupied as a separate dwelling by Mrs. Scott, née Elsie Middlemas, c. 1909. Pen and ink drawing by DSH, 1967.	43
A plan of estates at Countersett Hall and Holly House by W. Monkhouse, York, endorsed on a deed of 2 December, 1853. NYCRO, ZPM 30.	45
Semerdale House as it was built about 1812 but with bay windows of a later date. The third storey was taken off about 1898. Print by W. Monkhouse, York, from the Sale Catalogue of 1862 in the author's collection.	51
A plan of Semerdale House and grounds as drawn and endorsed on a deed of 29 December, 1862. Semerdale Deeds.	52
Boar Inn date stone showing the Latin inscription 'NUNC MEA MOX HUIUS SED POSTEA NESCIO CUIUS' which translates as, 'now mine, once thine, but whose afterwards I do not know'. Also the initials of Bartholomew and Isabell Harrison and the date 1667. Pen and ink drawing by DSH, 1979.	55
Bainbridge Friends Meeting House with original windows, a stove pipe and chimney stacks on both gables. There is a stable in the paddock with yew trees and holly bushes in the graveyard. c. 1890. Reproduced by permission of the Library Committee of London Yearly Meeting of the Religious Society of Friends.	60
Hawes Friends Meeting House with Meetings for Worship every Sunday at 10.30 am and 6.30 pm, 'All Seats Free', and an Adult School for men every Sunday at 4.30 pm. Photograph by Norman Penney [?] c. 1886. Reproduced by permission of the Library Committee of London Yearly Meeting of the Religious Society of Friends.	62
A sketch plan of the Friends Meeting House and Burial Ground at Hawes. The Burial Ground remains but the Meeting House was demolished in 1955. It stood about 20 yards south-east of the present fire station where the road now lies. Pen and ink drawing by DSH, 1988.	64
Countersett Friends Meeting House plan showing the layout of 1778 with the Elders' bench and ministers' gallery. The pulpit was installed by Methodists. Note pine panelling throughout, two ranks of loose benches, blocked doorways and windows from earlier buildings and flagstones set into the wooden floor where the stoves stood. Pen and ink drawing by DSH, 1977.	65
Countersett Friends Meeting House interior as completed in 1778 with the preacher's pulpit used by Primitive Methodists a century later. Photopgraph by William and Joan (Hunter) Hodgson, Northallerton, 1974.	65
The Friends' school at Countersett as constructed about 1772. It had a stable in the basement from the beginning and a flagged courtyard from 1861. Photograph by DSH, 1967.	70

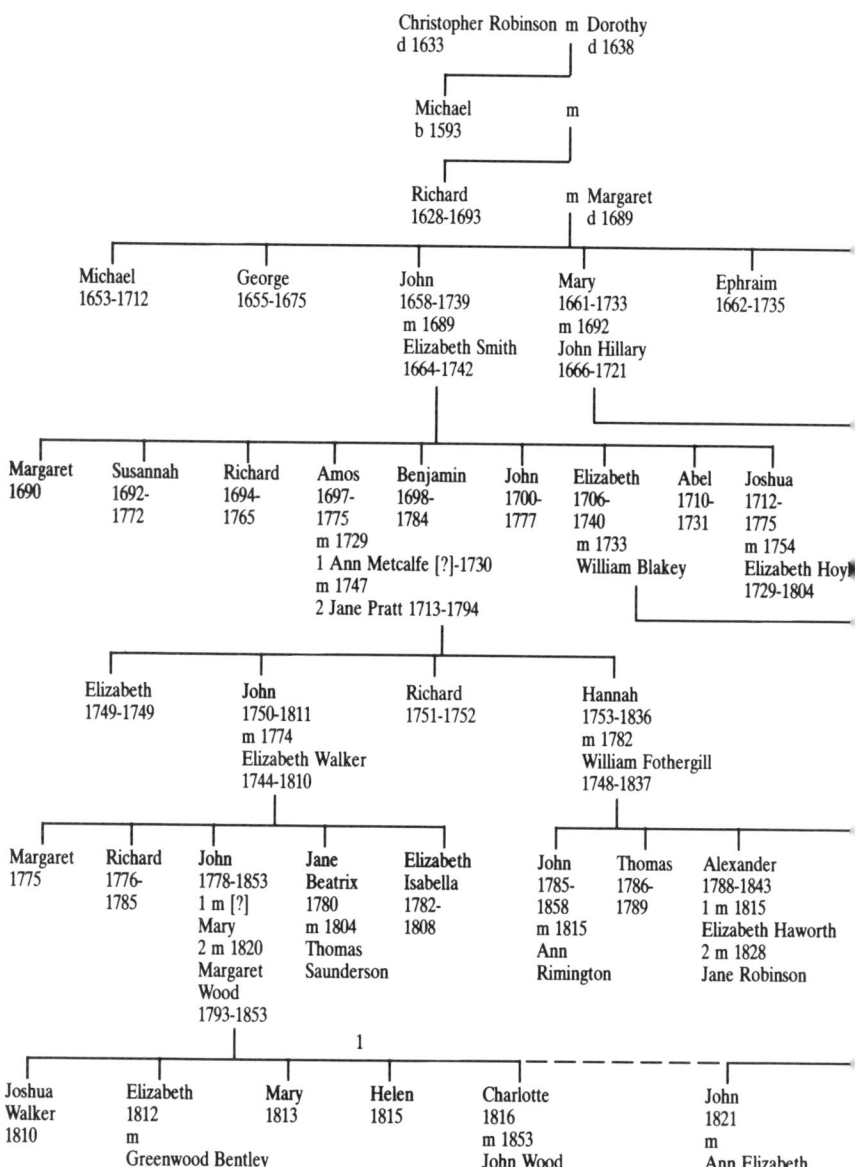

| Edward 1665 | Emanuel 1668 | child 1671-1671 | Rebecca 1672-1672 | Rachel 1673-1759 |

| Ann 1693 | Isaac 1694-1783 | Margaret 1695-1695 | Dau. 1696-1696 | John 1697 | William 1697-1763 | Margaret 1699 | Mary 1702-1755 | Richard 1703 | Rachel 1705-1773 |

Children of Wm Blakey but born after Elizabeth Robinson Blakey's death. Mother not found.

| John c 1734 c 1820 m [?] Mary 1749-1835 | Joshua 1736-1800 m 1766 Mary Beezon | William 1759 | Mary 1764 |

| Margaret 1789 c 1879 | Jane 1793 c 1883 m 1828 Thomas Whaley | John 1767 m 1786 Eleanor Dickinson | Richard 1769-1845 | Ann 1774 m 1793 James Thwaite | Elizabeth 1776 m 1802 Michael Fryer | Joshua Robinson 1779-1845 m Alice 1781-1856 | William 1784-1856 m Ann 1792-1853 | Thomas 1790-1848 m 1812 Margaret Fothergill 1786-1822 |

2

| William Hesp 1823-1823 | Richard 1824-1867 | Isabella 1825-1826 | Henry Wood 1829-1899 (Australia) | Thomas Wood 1830-1832 | Jeffery Wood 1831 (Australia) | Amos 1835 |

Acknowledgements

I THANK THE MANY OWNERS, archivists, librarians and individuals who have given me access to manuscripts, printed books and photographs used throughout this study, also all those who have discussed various aspects of the work over the years. I am particularly indebted to Richmond Monthly Meeting of the Society of Friends for the use of its important archive; to Michael Ashcroft, with present and past members of staff at the North Yorkshire County Record Office; to Edward Milligan and Malcolm Thomas and their staff at Friends House Library; to Dr. Arthur Raistrick for the Foreword; and to my wife June for unfailing support, encouragement and help with proof reading.

This publication has been made possible by generous grants from the Edith M. Ellis Trust, the W. F. Southall Trust, the Sir James Reckitt Charity, Richmond Monthly Meeting Trusts, and Jean Dower. The assistance of Peter Leyland as Treasurer of Richmond Monthly Meeting, and Margot Sessions and the team at William Sessions the Publishers is gratefully acknowledged.

DAVID S. HALL
Unicorn House
Bainbridge

Foreword

A STUDENT OF QUAKER HISTORY looking into most of the standard Quaker histories will find little mention of Wensleydale in the index. The common, and often the only, reference is to the passage of George Fox through the Dale on his journey from Pendle Hill to Sedbergh in June 1652. In recent literature there is little except Edmund Cooper's charming outline of *Quakerism in Wensleydale*. Now David Hall has given us a full and well-documented account of the life and work of the first Quaker in the Dale, Richard Robinson, set against a history of six generations of the Robinson family and their work as members of the Society of Friends.

Richard Robinson did not meet Fox but was convinced with Thomas Taylor, leader of the group of Seekers at Preston Patrick and visiting minister to the Seekers in Swaledale. Robinson became an eager preacher of the group of First Publishers of Truth, and travelled over much of the North Country establishing Quaker groups in many places. David's analysis of George Fox's journey through the Dales to Sedbergh is a new and very clear account of this old-standing problem of Quaker history.

The first Meetings in Wensleydale were held in Countersett Hall, Richard's home. One of the first Meeting Houses was built to adjoin it and it still stands and is in occasional use today.

For six generations the Robinson family was a powerful influence in the Quaker life of Wensleydale and Swaledale, building Meeting Houses, counselling Friends in many affairs, establishing charities and taking an important part in Monthly Meeting. Unfortunately with the increase in prosperity and the accumulation of property the later generations of the family drifted from their Quaker simplicity, built stylish houses and found their place in the Anglican communion.

This book is a well documented contribution to what has been a very inadequately recorded area of Quaker activity. We are grateful for the years of research that have gone into its compilation.

Linton, North Yorkshire, 1989   ARTHUR RAISTRICK

Introduction

THIS STUDY GREW OUT OF A DESIRE to know more than the guide books said about Countersett Hall, the author's home from 1951 to 1968. It is presented in four parts. The first deals with Richard Robinson (1628-93), his life as a yeoman at Countersett and his work among the early Quakers. Part two records the Robinson family fortunes through the next five generations. Their time in the Dale and association with Friends is shown against a background of social change, as they join the professions and aspire to gentry status. Then comes their final break with Wensleydale. The third and fourth parts are devoted to the buildings associated with the Robinson story – the four principal dwellings at Countersett, the Meeting House and school there, and the Meeting Houses at Hawes and Bainbridge.

The result is the compilation of a history of the house, the farm and the people who have lived and worked there throughout the last three centuries. During the research the study widened to include related properties, people and institutions with which the various occupiers of Countersett Hall were concerned. That Richard Robinson, who built the house, and the Society of Friends, the religious body to which he belonged, should loom large is inevitable, as Richard was the first Quaker in Wensleydale.

Much of this story centres on Raydaleside, the name given to the area surrounding Semerwater, the natural lake from which the short River Bain flows to join the River Yore, in the main valley of Wensleydale. The hamlets of Countersett, Marsett and Stalling Busk are set around Semerwater with single outlying farms completing the community.

The influence of Quakerism is evident throughout Richard's life and work. It was the faith which he adopted early and pursued vigorously all his life, setting an example for future generations to follow. He was a man of his time, that period known as the English Revolution. Political, religious and secular disorder ran out of control in the rise of sectarianism, the Civil War, the Commonwealth, the Restoration and the Glorious Revolution; the time when Englishmen experienced freedom of choice for themselves. Those who chose individualism took charge of their own destiny for the first time.

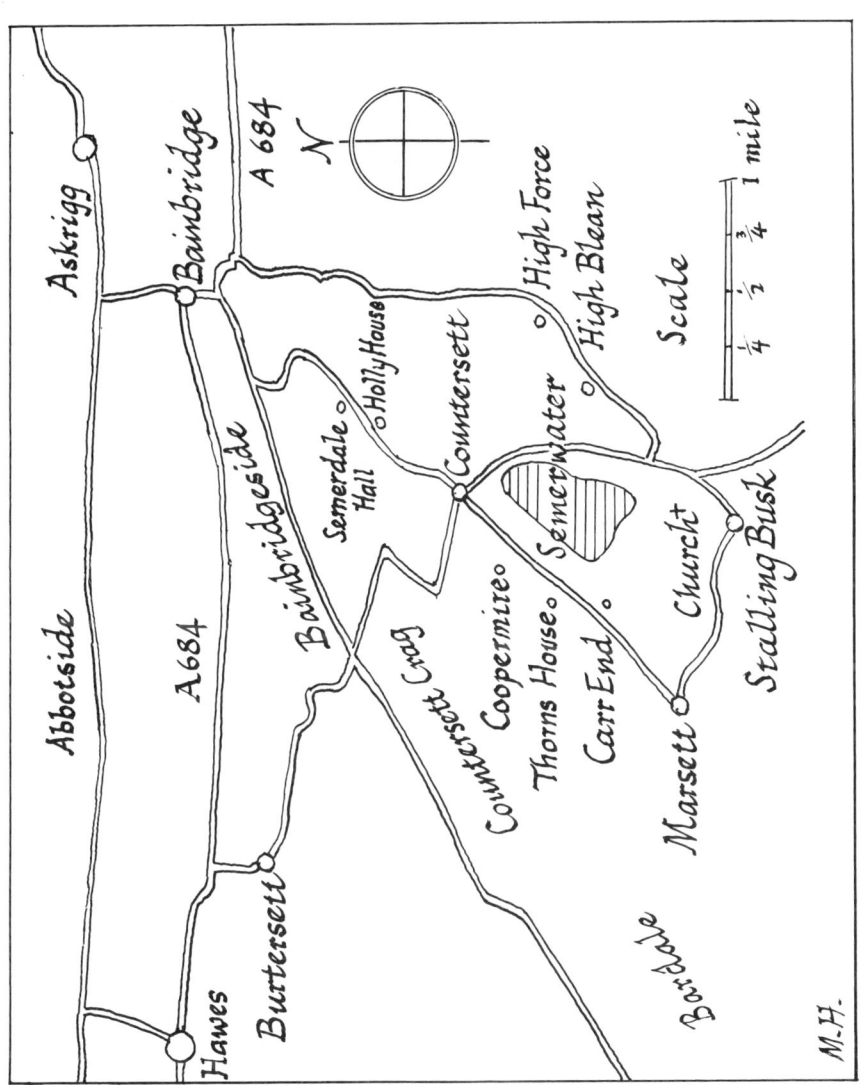

The area around Semerwater, known as Raydaleside. Here are the farms, hamlets and common pastures associated with the Robinson family story. Hawes and Bainbridge, like Countersett, were early centres of Quakerism.

The early history of the Quaker movement in Wensleydale is incomplete but there is evidence to suggest considerable activity among groups of Quaker-like separatists in Westmorland, Richmond and the West Riding of Yorkshire. It has been suggested that George Fox deliberately sought out sectarians on his journey in 1652 and the route he took tends to reinforce that claim. As Winthrop S. Hudson wrote in 1944 'he knew where to go and whom to see'.[1] He set out to contact and if possible to convince and unite dispersed groups of like-minded people. Fox came to Yorkshire, on foot, in the summer of 1652 via Pendle Hill. From there he struck out north and east, aiming perhaps for Richmond but got no further than Wensleydale from where he was drawn west to Sedbergh and Westmorland. Reconstructing in detail the route as given him in his Journal is very difficult. The main difficulties are the degree of reliability of a Journal written 22 years after the events it describes[2]; the scant amount of topographical evidence in it vis-a-vis locations and dates; the apparent length of daily journeys (some of 30 miles) including Meetings on the way; and that the account of the event in *The First Publishers of Truth* does not agree with that in the Journal.

The most likely route and dates are set out below with those places which are mentioned in the Journal as quotations and the remainder supplied from recent map and fieldwork.

1652, Tuesday, 1 June (18 miles). Whilst travelling north with Richard Farnsworth, Fox climbed 'Pendle Hill' and descended by a spring or stream on the north side, perhaps to Sawley or Grindleton where there was a group of dissenters known as Grindletonians.

Wednesday, 2 June (30 miles). The whole of this day spent 'among the fell countries' of Bowland, Ribblesdale, Malhamdale, Wharfedale and Coverdale, perhaps using the old roads via Mastiles Lane and Park Rash. The night was spent on a common among 'ferns or brackens' and probably in Coverdale.

Thursday, 3 June (27 miles). In the morning the two men moved on to a town, Middleham?, from where Fox continued alone 'up Wensleydale' to Askrigg and Bainbridge and an alehouse beyond. At Askrigg he saw the Thursday Market in progress, spoke in the church and passed on 'up the dales' to a schoolhouse, possibly at Yorebridge End. Later that day he wandered to an alehouse 'upon a common' near Bainbridge or Hawes and spent the night there.[3] The Robinson family's account of this day states distinctly, perhaps pointedly, that Fox neither spoke nor spent a night in the Dale at this time.[4] The conflicting reports cannot be reconciled on the evidence available at present.

Friday, 4 June (30 miles). Fox moved on 'through other dales' to 'John Blayking's' relations who remain unidentified, and over the tops to John

Tennant's 'Scarhouse in Langstroth Dale' and 'Dent' where he met the Mason family at Stonehouse. He slept that night at 'Major Bousfield's in Garsdale'.

Saturday, 5 June (30 miles). This day in Garsdale, 'Grizedale and several other dales', probably Cautley, Mallerstang, Ravenstonedale, or Howgill and so to 'Brigflatts' and Richard Robinson's house.

The following day, being Whit Sunday, Fox attended the separatists' meeting at Borratt, the home of Gervase Benson, near Brigflatts. On 9 June he spoke in Sedbergh churchyard, beside the market place on Fair Day; on Sunday 13 June he addressed a large assembly on the top of Firbank Fell near the old chapel; and on 16 June he attended the separatists' regular monthly meeting at Preston Patrick chapel. The Society of Friends recognise this group of meetings as constituting the foundation of their church. George Fox visited Yorkshire on at least eighteen occasions[5] and was in the vicinity of Wensleydale on five, but mentions it only in 1652 and 1677.[6]

It must be accepted that Fox did not meet Richard Robinson in 1652, for such an event would not have been forgotten by Richard's family who also had the account of his convincement, now lost, but 'Left by him in Manuscript for the benefit of his Children'.[7] Once convinced he set out to convert those of his neighbours who would listen and to establish regular Quaker Meetings in the Dale. He travelled widely in the north and is known to have spoken publicly at Askrigg, Carperby, Coverdale, Middleham, Wensley, Aysgarth, Grinton, Marrick, Marske, Hudswell, Hawes Chapel, Richmond, Easby, Gilling, Barnard Castle, Bishop Auckland, Darlington, Stockton, Yarm, Thirsk, Easingwold, Northallerton, Bedale, Ripon, Masham, Mashamside, Hubberholme, Settle, Kirkby Lonsdale, Westmorland, Kirkby Stephen, York Minster and the churchyard, York Assizes and Quarter Sessions, Nottingham, London, the Court of Exchequer, Westminster Hall, Cheapside, Leadenhall Market, St. Pauls and the churchyard, 'Horsecourses & Cock fightings and many by places'.[8]

When at home Richard compiled his Meeting's record of Quaker 'Suffering's' in respect of imprisonment and distraint for unpaid tithe and church rates, etc., to which all Quakers objected as a matter of principle. He published at least two pamphlets on Quaker sufferings 'for Truth' in the Dales, and wrote long erudite letters which combined questions of faith and business. He appears to have acted as chief legal adviser to Philip Swale in respect of lead mines and to have continued all his literary and business activities even when in prison.

It is often difficult to identify Richard Robinson and his work precisely because there were at least four other men of that name active among Quakers in the north in his time. They include Richard Robinson of Healaugh Park who married Mary Pratt at Kearton in 1659, raised a large family in Swaledale, and died there in 1680. Richard Robinson of Brigflatts, who married Mary Blaykling from Drawell in 1649, met Fox in 1652, was imprisoned in London for tithe, died and was buried at Brigflatts in 1673. Richard Robinson of High Burton near Masham, who belonged to Masham Meeting, died and was buried at Low Ellington in 1672, and Richard Robinson of Roecliffe, who was held captive in York Castle during the 'Great Imprisonment' and baptised a child at Aldborough church in 1667.[9]

There is no portrait of Richard Robinson extant: such things were considered vain by early Quakers. Nor is there a detailed description of his personal appearance. Early accounts were concerned more with moral and spiritual characteristics. In old age he was the most venerable member of Richmond Monthly Meeting and his presence at Richmond Preparative Meeting was minuted twice, a most unusual occurrence and a measure of the regard in which he was held locally.

> 1st 3m 1684. Friends this day mett, & our Friend R.R. being here also, we injoyed a Good oppertunity together. [And] At our Monethly Meeting att Richmond the 5th of 7mo. [16]89 divers friends this day Mett as usuall, & injoyed a good oppertunity together (R.R. being then present) but no business was offered to the consideration of friends, but matters left to the next Monthly Meeting, if ought shall then happen needfull to offer to friends.[10]

John Fothergill of Carr End (1675-1744) was active in the Wensleydale Meeting and wrote of 'an ancient and truly valuable Minister' there who died in 1692/3, almost certainly Richard Robinson. Fothergill thought his virtues lay in 'his faithfulness, his waiting to feel after, and adhering to that manifestation of divine power and life from almighty God, whereof he declared; that this principle, to which he laboured to turn and gather peoples minds appeared in all, and as hereby he was made truly serviceable'.[11]

The succeeding generations of Quaker Robinsons, though acting in many respects much as Richard had done, began to assume a different outlook. They were much less outgoing, concentrating more on improving their worldly status, on rebuilding their homes and Meeting Houses yet, initially at least, retaining an active interest in all things Quaker. For two generations more they were content to remain in their native place where they grew rich amid a body of like-minded people, led first by John and then by Amos Robinson. They moved and married within a close group of Quaker families including Fothergill, Blakey, Thwaite, Hillary, Metcalfe, Pratt, Binks, Harrison, Lambert, Routh and Thompson. By the 1750s the Quakers had become an acknowledged exclusive sect, a situation dramatically opposed to that of their early days and one harbouring danger for the future. Amos Robinson, a minister from 1736, was heard 'often expressing a Sorrow for the low Situation of the Church, and that so few of the rising Generation were desirous to follow the Example of our worthy Elders'.[12]

John Robinson (1750-1811) as a fourth generation Quaker changed course completely. His wealth and education allowed him to forsake his farming roots and forge for himself a career in medicine in Bradford. The farms were let to tenants and the Robinsons henceforth would, for the most part, be absentee landlords relying heavily on rents and capital reserves. The strictures of Friends became too much and the fifth generation Robinson 'married out', that is married a person not in membership of the Society of Friends.

Thereafter the family assumed the lifestyle of gentlefolk over reliant on capital and mortgages which led, it seems, to a cash crisis and the demise of the Robinsons as landowners and their disappearance from Countersett. In many respects their fortunes are typical of several early Quaker families including Fothergill, Blakey and Thwaite who came to the faith early, throve on a combination of zeal and industry and thus acquired riches which allowed later generations to emigrate and finally outreach their resources. Of the old Quaker families that of Thwaite alone remains in Wensleydale but they lost their links with Raydaleside and the Society of Friends generations ago.

Every historical study is shaped by the availability of sources and this one is no exception. The absence of a Robinson family archive is unfortunate and not wholly rectified by the exceptionally good set of records preserved by Richmond Monthly Meeting. This led to research in a mass of related material for gleams of light on the family and their times. There are notable gaps, especially in the case of Richard Robinson, for whom a 'Life' was never written. Neither his wife nor his mother are known, nor are the date and details of his marriage which may well predate his convincement. Nothing of his education is recorded.

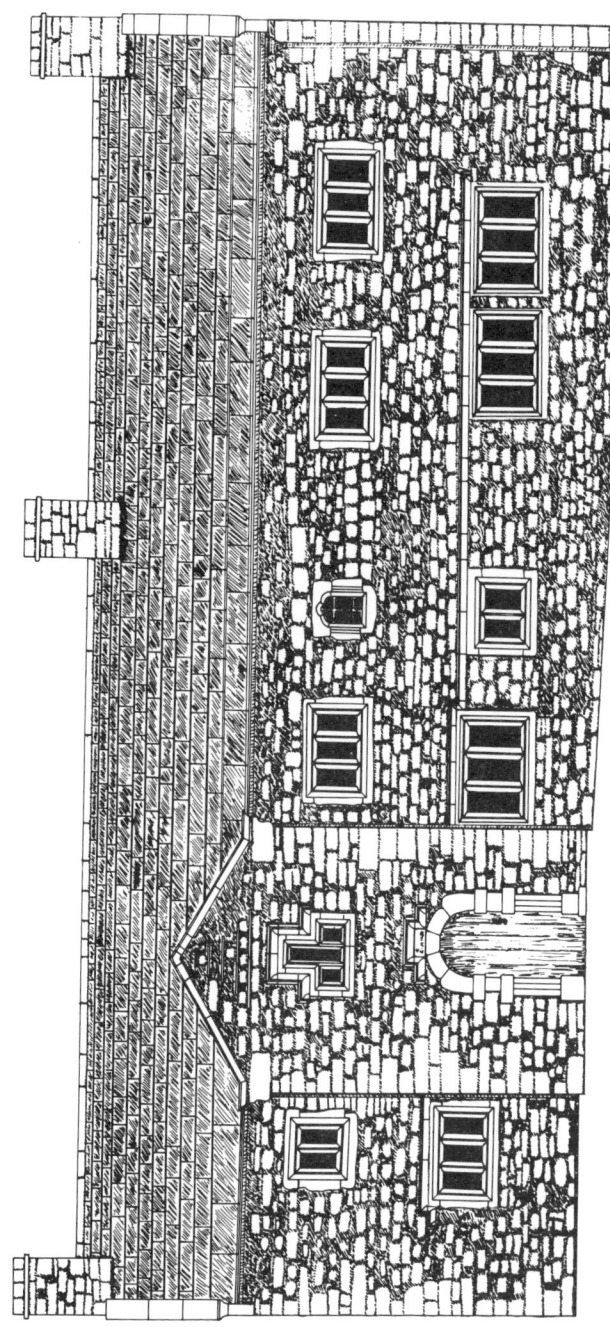

Countersett Hall as it was in Richard Robinson's time with three mullioned windows restored from surviving evidence.

PART I

The First Quaker in Wensleydale

The Man Convinced

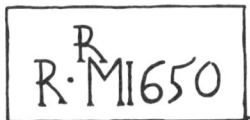

Countersett Hall date stone showing the initials of Richard and Margaret Robinson and the date 1650.

RICHARD ROBINSON (1628-93) came of a family long established in Wensleydale. The parish registers for Castle Bolton, Redmire and Wensley contain numerous Robinson entries and the same christian names were used for generations: John, William, Christopher, Michael, Charles and Leonard were common. A rarity, for example, was Reynard.[1] Richard's grandfather was Christopher and he may well have been the Christopher Robinson, who with Michael Robinson, perhaps his brother, was described as a yeoman of Redmire when they purchased lands near that village, 'formerly part of [the] monastery of Coverham and tenanted by Symon Robinson,' in 1580.[2] Christopher Robinson raised a large family of six sons and five daughters, the eldest of whom was Michael christened in 1593.[3] Michael married 'an Heiris, a Consientious & Tender Spirited woman' whose name has not been recorded. Richard was their only child. The family belonged to the established church so when the boy was born, at Preston under Scar in the summer of 1628,[4] he was baptised in the parish church at Wensley. The register states briefly 'Richardus filius Michaelis Robinson 3 die Septembris'.[5] As Richard grew to sturdy manhood he developed an unusually serious mind and 'was brought up a Schol[a]r (but not in the Universities)'.[6] Events were to prove his education sound, with a strong

1

tendency towards the law but whether there is sufficient evidence to describe him as a lawyer is open to debate.

A strong religious curiosity led him to many priests and professors but 'haveing Inspected them all, . . . he could find no true satisfaction amongst any of them'. An account of his state at this time describes him 'as a specled Bird in the wilderness, or as an owle in the Desert, or sparrow upon the housetop'. Rumour of George Fox's preaching was rife and Richard, for all that he had not met the man, joined him 'in his mind'.[7] In point of fact he had been drawn to Thomas Taylor, a dissenting minister from Carleton in Craven who was leading a group of separatist 'Seekers' at Preston Patrick in Westmorland and a body of like minded people in Richmond and Swaledale.[8] That was the position in May 1652 when George Fox made his momentous first journey through the Dales. He did not visit Countersett and did not meet Richard Robinson on that occasion. He passed on quickly to Sedbergh and the Fell country beyond, where he achieved instant success. Fox gathered the large company of Seekers there almost wholly to 'The Children of the Light', the first name used by Friends.[9]

When word of this reached Wensleydale, Richard Robinson set off for Westmorland. He went first to a Meeting of Fox's followers at Francis Howgill's house at Todthorne, near Grayrigg then to one at Hutton which was being led by John Audland and John Snowdon. And there, with his friend Thomas Taylor present, he saw that George Fox's teaching opened the way to true salvation. He was convinced, and dedicated his life to 'Truth' in the service of God. When he returned to Countersett, his home became the principal meeting place for Quakers in the Dale and the frequent resort of travelling preachers.[10]

Richard Hubberthorne from Yealand Redmayne, 'dear innocent Richard' as George Fox was to describe him in later years, was the first to come and together these two zealous youthful Quakers set out to convince Wensleydale.[11] They met with considerable success but were not always well received. They were abused at Carperby and at Askrigg, where Richard Robinson would be well known. 'Many of the People were Exceding Rude'. Nevertheless, during those few weeks in the winter of 1652-3 they established a Preparative Meeting which functions to this day.[12]

The true extent of Richard's work as an itinerant preacher is uncertain but he certainly became a familiar figure throughout the northern counties. There was hardly a town or village between York and Newcastle which did not hear him 'proclaiming the Truth' in the church, the market place or the court house. He was in London on at least two occasions and spoke publicly there and in Westminster.[13] 'He travelled much on foot', we are told, 'being a lusty, strong man of body, and likewise finding it to be more agreeable to his service in those public places, the roughness of the people in those times considered, for he was forced to lay sometimes out of doors in the fields, and to travel in the night as well as the day, and in winter seasons as well as summer, without shrinking from the violence of weather. And after this manner the Lord led him on his way through many rough and untrodden paths: but the Lord's power was with him and supported him through them all; and notwithstanding the many blows and strokes he got by staves and clubs, several of which were broken upon him with such violence that pieces thereof flew up into the air.'[14]

A strong personality is shown by his going naked through the streets as a sign of the naked truth after the fashion of the Old Testament prophet Isiah. Action of this sort was by no means as uncommon as we might think and several Friends are known to have 'performed the Service'. Richard went to Askrigg steeplehouse, 'Sometimes in his shift'; to Middleham many times, 'once in his Shift on a market day'; and to Richmond several times 'where he was sore bett, and had urine thrown upon him being in his shift'. Such behaviour brought ridicule and comtempt upon the individual concerned and the Society of Friends as a whole. The practice was soon abandoned.[15]

Countersett from a postcard showing the Hall with pointing fresh from the alterations of 1885. Note the tall chimney on Elsie House, the White House coloured white and the Board Inn (also white) with its signboard prominently displayed.

Such is the background of Richard Robinson's spiritual enlightenment. He married early and with his wife Margaret established himself on a farm at Countersett in the high Dales. The small inscribed stone above the door of the house at Countersett Hall records the event as R·RM 1650 and here Richard and Margaret raised a family of six sons and three daughters, Michael (1653), George (1655), John (1658), Mary (1661), Ephraim (1662), Edward (1665), Emanuel (1668), Rebecca (1672) and Rachel (1673).[16] Michael became a yeoman at Countersett but never married and George died in Jamaica. John farmed Semerdale and left an heir and Mary married John Hillery of Birk Rigg. Ephraim lived as a bachelor at Holly House, Edward has not been traced and Emanuel was mentally deficient. A still-born child was buried in Richard's ground at Countersett in 1671 and the following year the infant Rebecca was buried in Friends Burial Ground at Bainbridge. Rachel never married but she became and remained a prominent and resourceful member of Wensleydale Meeting until she died aged 86 years in 1759.

When Richard Robinson first came to Countersett it was as a tenant of the City of London, whose civic body had purchased the Manor of Bainbridge from the Crown in 1628. He paid a fee farm rent of almost £5 per annum which shows his to have been the largest holding of any tenant in Bainbridge or Raydaleside.[17] The rental for Michaelmas 1661 shows him among his immediate neighbours.

Countersett Moneyes received at ye Audit held ye 14th of Octobr 1661

	£	s	d
of Richard Robinson for ½ yeare	2	9	7½
of John Metcalfe		7	6
of Anthony Thwaytes		12	6
of James Taylor		11	10½
of Edmond Harrison			1
of Richard Hills		1	4
of John Lancaster		18	7
of Allex: Metcalfe		4	9
Sume is	5	6	3 [18]

Richard was in possession of the freehold later but the original conveyance to him has not been discovered, nor indeed has the indenture of 1660-1 'between Richard Robinson of the one part and Francis Smithson of the other part' which was mentioned in a schedule of the Semerdale deeds c.1862.[19]

Richard is generally thought of today as a yeoman but when he and 10 men all of similar standing in the Dale purchased the manorial rights for Bainbridge in 1663 they were all described as Gentlemen.[20] The move to secure these privileges to the inhabitants was inspired and to a large extent engineered by Richard Robinson. He arranged the purchase and collected the money, part of which was raised by a capital levy on the tenants in proportion to their rents. His account of monies gathered from every hamlet[21] is preserved along with his account for personal expenses connected with the purchase. Several items from the latter are presented here to illustrate his involvement. The document is endorsed 'An Acc[ou]nt of my fathers jo[u]rney to London about the Deed of the Royal[t]ies'.

> The Royalties of Bainbridge Contracted for the 8th of August in the yeare 1658 Cost £214. 11. 11. of w[hi]ch there was p[ai]d in hand £21. 11. 11. the rest being the sume of 193 was due the 11th day of November 1658. . . .
> Cuth: Wynn and my selfe up to London our Charges ther whyle Cuth: staid and his down againe £6. 9. 3. . . .
> My owne Charges after Cuth: left me and laid out about getting the deed sealed in wine and stronge water and sending twise into the Cuntry to gett it sealed to the servants where I lay coming home for lett & Carrage of my things to Richmond and other matters £7. 0. 3. . . .
> My horse after Cuth: left me as I remember £3. 7. 6. . . .
> My Charges in Goeing up to London againe my Charges whylest I stayed there Twenty shill for a horse to ride down on Charges in seeking of Records Court roles and my charges in Coming downe againe £3. 18. 8. . . .
> My last jorney up to London of this cost £9. 16. 8.[22]

By 1650 the City was eager to realise its interests in the Wensleydale lands. Many of the tenants were able to buy their own farms and for all that the details are not forthcoming we must assume that Richard was one of them. This new found freedom encouraged many new freeholders to undertake a complete renovation of their old, sometimes ling-thatched farmhouses, thereby bringing a wealth of mid-17th century architecture to the Dales. Richard almost rebuilt his. By extending it to the east he added two large rooms, one above the other each with a good stone arched fireplace and a fine oak floor between them. Six three-light ogee mullioned windows and a single light trefoil headed one were inserted on the front but the older splayed mullions of the earlier house were retained at the west end and at the back. These and other features typical of the period, including a fine carved oak door, have survived subsequent alterations. The house would then appear much as we know it today with the large two storey porch, which, though not locked to the main house, is with its individual window, labels and kneelers, part of Richard's rebuilding. In 1673 he was taxed on five hearths.[23] The same number survive in the house today.

Farming records have not survived from Richard's day but later documents show his farm to have been something in the region of 180 acres of old enclosed land north of Countersett with extensive grazing rights on the unenclosed Crag, Bardale and Bainbridgeside pastures.[24] Here he kept ten milk cows and a bull, four twinter beasts, eight stirks, nine calves, six horses, sixty-three ewes and three tups, twenty-five shear wethers and forty-six hogs. Much of the hay crop was stacked in the fields but several 'Peeces' were stored in buildings nearer home. There were 'Pultry' in the garth and three beehives in the garden.[25]

Continuing Faith

By 1664 George Fox and his followers had organised Meetings throughout the northern counties and within a few years the remainder of Britain was settled in Meetings. There is no accurate record of the Quakers' strength at that time but it has been estimated as from thirty to forty thousand out of a total population of around five million.[1] Religious minorities, especially unconventional ones, are never popular with the authorities and the Quakers were no exception. Their obstinate and at times outlandish behaviour led them into trouble and at times of national unrest they were always suspect.

One such occasion was the Fifth Monarchy Rising of January, 1661 when a panic wave swept the country and carried thousands of Quakers into prison where they were held, suspected of complicity in the rebellion. Some 500 were herded into the Castle at York and kept there for about four months. Henry Jackson from Wooldale in West Yorkshire[2] was one of them and he spent part of his time confined with Richard Robinson 'in a great Oven which stood in the Castle yard wall'.[3] Richard was not there as a suspect rebel but:

> because he would not pay Tythes was cast in prison by Christopher Clapham about the 2^d of the 12th moneth 1660 [Feb. 1661] where he lay about a quarter of a year and then released by his wives father who paid as was said for his Sufferhage £10 or a cow wherby w[i]thout the consent or knowledge of the said Richard.[4]

The Rising was to have serious and far reaching consequences in the 'Clarendon Code', a series of Parliamentary Acts, that were directed against sectarians in general and Quakers in particular. This led to almost 30 years of ruthless persecution and exploitation of Friends. The first prosecutions in Wensleydale took place in the autumn of 1662. Richard, needless to say, was deeply involved and left a detailed account.

> Upon the 31st Day of the 6th Moneth, called August, in the Year 1662. being the first Day of the Week, came James Metcalfe of Nappa, in the County of York, and then in the Commission of Peace

to the Door of James Wetherald in Askrigg in the same County, where some of the People of God in Scorn called Quakers were peaceably met together, only to wait upon and worship the One, True and Living God in Spirit and Truth, according to his will and those manifestations of him they had received. And though he the said James Metcalfe had often known or heard of their so peaceably meeting together at that place before that time, and for no other purpose save only (as aforsaid) to wait upon and worship the Lord; yet to the intent to render the said People more Odious or Dangerous, or else to render his Appearance the more Terrible, he brought with him a great Company of Armed men; and being on this wise come to the Door of the said House, they caused Friends by the said Armed men to be had out, and brought before them; where upon Promise made to appear before the said James Metcalfe the next day, they all, save Richard Robinson, let go, and him the said James Metcalfe commited to the Custody of Richard Besson of the same Askrigg, then Constable, who let him go Home also: and coming again the next day, the said James Metcalfe commited Nineteen of them to the Common Jayle at York, and Four to the House of Correction, untill the next Quarter Sessions of the Peace, to be held for the North-Riding of the said County of York. But by the Kindness of the said Constable, Rich Besson, to whose Charge they were commited, they stayed at Home most part of a Moneth; and then through Threatnings of the said James Metcalfe, sent to Prison untill the said Sessions, where, after much Discourse those Persons here-after-named, with others, were fined, and the Fines levied as followeth.

First, Richard Robinson of Countersett in Wensleydale was fined 2£. for which he had a Mare distrained by Christopher Todd of Middleham, Edmond Blades and Bartholomew Blades of Askrigg, aforesaid, or some of them, about the 3d day of the 11 moneth, in the Year 1662. worth, by the Owners Estimation of her, 3£. 6s. 8d.

Richard Rowth of Hawes was fined 10s. for which the aforesaid Persons, or some of them, did distrain and take a Cow, at or about the same time, worth about 3£. 10s.

Bartholomew Harryson of Countersett and Isabell his Wife, being fined either of them 12d. had distrained for the same by the aforesaid Persons, or some of them, about the time aforesaid, some Cloth and Apparel, but the same was released by a Neighbour, and returned back again, only the party got some other Commodities, and stayed so much as the Fines came to, in Payment for the same.

James Gurnell of Marsett, fined 10s. had four Pewter Dishes and one Riding Coat distrained, and taken for the same, by the aforesaid Edmond and Bartholomew Blaydes, the 13th day of the Moneth aforesaid, worth 1£. 9s.

Mary Lambert of Busk fined 10s. had Stockings distrained and taken for the same, by the aforesaid Edmond and Bartholomew Blaydes, worth about 12s.

There were several other Persons at that time fined, besides what is beforementioned, so that the Fines in all came to 19£. 13s. But whether any of the Residue was distrained for or no, I know not.[5]

The record of the Quarter Sessions held at Thirsk 27 October, 1662 disagrees in part with Richard's account but it is clear that all the fines were distrained for, even those of a shilling. In 1663 the Justices ordered that money 'levied off Quakers according to an Act of Parliament' was to be paid to Thomas Nickolson, master of the House of Correction at Richmond 'to be employed for the stocke of the House'.[6] Richard and his friends were to know that particular house, at the west end of Newbiggin, very well in later years.

The 'Yorkshire Plot' of October, 1663, like the Fifth Monarchy Rising, was to have serious repercussions for Quakers and especially for those living in the western Dales. Some of the plotters came from the Dales and were, or had been Quakers.[7] Richard Robinson was in London at the time, concluding negotiations for the purchase of Bainbridge Manor. He was examined at his lodging, the Bear Inn, Basinghall Street, behind the Guildhall. It emerged that he knew Thomas Atkinson, a Quaker, and the brothers John and George Atkinson of Askrigg.[8] John Atkinson was deeply involved in the Plot[9] but Richard was not. He did admit knowledge of John Atkinson and that they may have discussed the government whilst 'they lay together' in York Castle, but Richard was able to prove his innocence and so was discharged and allowed to make his way home with Thomas Hird, a drover from Craven who wished to travel with him. Nevertheless the upheaval was so great and the implications for Quakers so serious that George Fox found it necessary to issue a paper opposing the principle of plotting against authority.[10]

Richard was in trouble again in 1664, this time for refusing to pay his 'proportionable assessment towards the reparation of the Church and other holy uses being 3s. 8d. and also not cominge to the publique' worship at Askrigg Church.[11] The matter was brought to the notice of the Archdeacon and the Consistory Court but again the outcome is not known.

As the years went by the prosecutions increased in number and severity. James Metcalfe continued to issue many of the warrants against Quakers in the upper Dale, warrants that were as often as not based on information supplied by professional 'informers' who claimed one third of any fine imposed by a successful prosecution. At least five informers were operating in Wensleydale and Swaledale but William Thornaby senior, of Richmond was the most active. A detailed account of his activities in the early summer of 1670 has been preserved. He notes seven First Day Meetings held between 22 May and 3 July, the meeting place, the names of those present and the value of the fines imposed. Friends met once at Thomas Fawcett's house in Hawes, three times in Ann Coward's house at Bainbridge and three times on Bainbridge Pastures. This last place would avoid the statutory £20 inflicted on any convicted householder. Richard was present on four occasions and was suitably punished each time, first with a fine of £1, then £2 10s., £4 and finally £7. In all, 36 Friends were fined a total of £134 15s. in seven weeks.[12] This would bring Thornaby £44 18s. 4d., a most satisfactory outcome for him. We can perhaps appreciate Richard's feelings when he recalls having told him that the Lord would bring 'Ruin, Desolation or Destetution upon him, and his Family or House, . . . which shortly after came to pass'.[13]

Thornaby's information is useful for the light it throws on the individuals who were active in Quaker affairs in upper Wensleydale some 20 years after the Meeting was settled. They include:–

Isabel Atkinson	Thomas Nickolson, Bainbridge
Richard Atkinson	Michael Pratt, Broughill
Thomas Beedon, Hawes	Richard Robinson, Countersett
Elizabeth Binks	Alice Rowth
Mary Binks	Christopher Rowth, Hawes
Richard Binks, Hawes	Elizabeth Rowth, Bainbridge
Ann Coward, Bainbridge	Oswold Rowth, Hawes
Thomas Fawcett, Hawes	Richard Rowth, Hawes
Thomas Gibson, Stalling Busk	Seth Rowth
Barth: Harrison, Countersett	Thomas Rowth
Edward Harrison, Countersett	Mary Spence
Elizabeth Lambert	John Stockdale
Isabel Lambert	Jonas Stockdale
John Lambert	Francis Thompson, Marsett
Mary Lambert, Stalling Busk	James Thompson
William Mason	John Thompson, Blean
Ann Metcalfe	Dorothy Todd, Bainbridge
Francis Metcalfe, Mossdale	Isabel Williamson, Richmond[14]

The house called 'Ann Coward's' in Thornaby's record was the first proper Meeting House that Friends had in Wensleydale. It was described as a 'Cottage house situate lying and being in Bainbridge' when Elizabeth Routh and Dorothy Todd, as trustees bought it for the Society on 7 December, 1668.[15] Four years later Friends acquired 'One Pece or parcell of ground containing Twenty yards of square now measured out upon Holme-bray' for a Burial Ground.[16] Richard was involved with both transactions and was a trustee of the latter.

These were difficult years for the Quakers as a whole and for Richard there was the added burden of tragedy at home. Two children died in 1671 and 1672. In 1675 word came of the death of young George Robinson, the second son of the household who, with Richard Atkinson, had joined the stream of Quaker colonists. He died in Jamaica at the house of Elizabeth Reed and was buried in her ground at Lacova Savana, 4 August, 1675, aged 20.[17]

Nearer home Richard mortgaged 'All that messuage or dwelling house wherein one Stephen Tennant did then dwell and inhabit [1675] and all garths, closes and parcels of ground to the same belonging called . . . New Close and all them two closes of ground called the Tongues and four cattle gates in Bainbridgeside . . . [and] one close called West Close' with all woods, underwoods, etc. at Countersett, to Philip Swale of Hartforth, Robert Gosling of Richmond, John Chaytor and Thomas Johnson of the same place, in trust for the 'poor and needy Quakers in and about Richmond'. The mortgage was conveyed to new trustees in 1709 and 1738 and was finally paid off by Richard's great grandson in 1780.[18]

Richard's standing within the Society was clearly demonstrated when he was summoned to Westmorland as one of the nine Elders who would, it was hoped, bring about a settlement of the Wilkinson-Story clash which threatened to disrupt the entire Society of Friends. The interested parties met first at Poolbank in the Lythe valley and then at Milnthorpe in 1675 but without success. They met again the following spring for a four day conference at Drawell near Sedbergh but again they failed to bring about the desired reconciliation. George Fox remained the leader of the Society but it was very many years before the rumblings of discontent finally disappeared.[19]

The names of those most active in Quaker circles in Wensleydale were presented to the Consistory Court at Richmond in 1679 and 20 of them came from Raydaleside. They include Richard and Margaret Robinson and their sons Michael and John, with Bartholomew and Isabell Harrison and their sons Edward and John, Alexander Metcalfe and his son, all from Countersett; Alexander Fothergill from Carr End; James Gurnel, Jacob Thompson, Francis Thompson, Jane Gurnel and Margaret Metcalfe, all from Marsett; Thomas Calvert, Augustine and Anthony Metcalfe, all from Stalling Busk; and John Thompson from Blean.[20]

On 26 March, 1677 George Fox left Swarthmore Hall, near Ulverston for London on a prearranged route which brought him through the Yorkshire Dales. His health at the time was far from good. His wife, who accompanied him as far as Drawell near Sedbergh, wrote to one of her daughters from there on 31 March, 'Your father is not altogether as weary as he was, but he cannot endure to ride but very little journeys and lights often, but he is pretty well and hearty, praised be the Lord'.[21]

And so, in the early days of April, George Fox set off with Leonard Fell and Edward Haistwell for Richard Robinson's house at Countersett, the next stopping place on the journey. They travelled through Garsdale, 'Visitinge Friends as they went, and Leonard Fell stayed at a place called the Haws, where hee had a Meeting in the Evening'. Haistwell and Fox meanwhile passed on to 'Countersyde, where severall Friends came to visitt Him that night'.[22] These few cryptic remarks in Edward Haistwell's diary remain the sole evidence of George Fox's presence at Countersett Hall. Next morning a few local Friends came to Countersett and accompanied the party over the high and bleak Stake Road to Scarrhouse in Langstrothdale, 'The way many times deep and bad with snow and our horses sometimes were down, and we were not able to ride', wrote George from York a few days later.[23] For a man who could ride 'but very little journeys' this must have been a very trying experience. However, he was present at Scarrhouse next day declaring the truth for 'severall houres' to a large and joyful crowd of Friends from 'Wensydaile, & Littendaile, & Bishopsdaile, & Skipton, & Coverdaile, & from Kellet in Lancashire, & from Sedbergh etc'. The party moved on next day through Bishopdale to Middleham and Marmaduke Beckwith's house near Masham, the next stopping place on the journey to York.[24]

Sufferings and other Exercises

Joseph Craddock, Commissary to the Bishop of Chester struck the Quakers of Wensleydale a grievous blow when, on 4 January, 1679 he detained Richard Robinson, John Fothergill and Christopher Routh under writs of Excommunicato Capiendo. Stephen Winn and Richard Geldart from Carlton in Coverdale joined them in the House of Correction at Richmond soon after.

> The said Richard Robinson for Non-payment of an Assessment of 10d. imposed upon him towards the Repair of the Steeplehouse at Askrigg, and other Matters joyned with the same, as Money for Destroying of Foxes, & c, all which he could have paid save that for the Repair of the Steeplehouse, if the same had been distinctly assessed.
>
> John Fothergill for an assessment of 5s. imposed on him for the same Use, but never demanded on him (as he affirms) neither did he hear of the same until he was Arrested, which was very Unjust. It Had been but reasonable to demand or aquaint the party with what they expect from him, before they endeavour to punish for Non-payment of that which was never demanded of him.

Stephen Winne and Richard Geldart, for not going to the Steeplehouse, nor receiving the Sacrament (so called) or some such like things.[1]

A BLAST blown out of the NORTH

And Ecchoing up towards the

SOUTH,

To meet the CRY of their

Oppreſſed Brethren.

Being a Relation of ſome of the Sufferings and other Exerciſes of ſeveral of the People of God in ſcorn called *Quakers* in and about *Richmond, Maſſam, Coverdale, Wenſleydale* and *Swaledae*, and ſome others of the adjacent Parts and Places in the *North Riding* of the County of *York*, ſince the beginning of the year 1660.

Prov 10.7. *The Memory of the Juſt is Bleſſed; but the Name of the Wicked ſhall Rot.*
Job 18.7. *The Light ſhall be dark in his Tabernacle, and his Candle ſhall be put out with him.*
Verſ. 16. *His Roots ſhall be dryed up beneath, and above ſhall his Branch be cut off.*
Verſ. 17. *His Remembrance ſhall periſh from the Earth, and he ſhall have no Name in the Street.*
Verſ. 20. *They that come after him ſhall be aſtoniſhed at his Day, as thoſe that went before were afrighted.*
Verſ. 21. *Surely ſuch are the Dwellings of the Wicked, and thus is the Place of him that knoweth not God.*
Prov. 10.23. *It is a Sport to a Fool to do Miſchief; but a Man of Underſtanding hath Wiſdom.*
Verſ. 25. *As the whirlewind paſſeth, ſo is the Wicked no more; but the Righteous is an Everlaſting Foundation.*

Printed in the Year 1680.

Title page from A Blast blown out of the North *which Richard Robinson wrote in prison at Richmond and had published in 1680.*

Richard was held for about two years during which time he wrote two books. One was a doctrinal work entitled *A Warning to the Inhabitants Of the whole Earth*, which he wished to have read in Meeting 'From your Real Friend and A wellwisher to all men Richard Robinson'. The other was his better known *A Blast blown out of the North And Ecchoing up towards the South, to meet the Cry of their Oppressed Brethren*, already quoted. This had been drafted about 1672 as an account of Quaker suffering in and around Richmond, Masham, Coverdale, Wensleydale and Swaledale since the beginning of 1660 but as James Metcalfe died and William Thornaby had left for London the persecutions ceased and the publication was abandoned. Joseph Craddock resumed the harassment of Quakers so Richard revised his work which, when it finally appeared in 1680, ran to 45 closely printed pages.

Richard was released after some two years' confinement at Richmond. The circumstances surrounding his release are obscure but interesting. The records show 'Thomas Craddock, Joseph son, being a member of Parliament for the Town of Richmond, & one [Humphery] Wharton, of Gilling Wood Hall, the other Member for Richmond, & Knowing that the said Craddocks were bad, corrupt, p[er]secuting men, the said Wharton moved the said Richard Robinsons Case in the parliam[en]t-house, against Tho[mas] Craddock as being a p[er]secutor, whereupon the said Craddock being ashamed, & Rich[ar]d Robinson lying the matter close upon him by Letter, the said Craddock made way for Rich[ar]d Robinsons Releasem[en]t soon after'.[2] Philip Swale wrote to Thomas Taylor c. 15 January, 1681, 'All those that were prisoners have except C. Rowth were by means of Tho[mas] Craddock (whome RR. writ to, & layd their case before him) discharged the 29 of the 10 Moneth last'.[3]

George Fox urged his followers to keep accurate records of Meetings, members, business, property transactions and the like. Thus, Quakers are a thoroughly documented sect. We may wonder if this was discussed at Countersett in 1677 for within a few years we find Friends opening a stout book bound in vellum with paper leaves and bright green tapes as 'A Book Intended to contain the Records of things taken note of and from time to time Agreed unto and Resolved in the particular Monthly Meeting of friends in Wensleydale Meeting'.[4] The Meeting had functioned for almost 30 years during which time it had developed a dozen or more active centres up and down the Dale and a mid-week Monthly Meeting which acted as the executive body for them all. This was always held at Countersett and the first entry begins, 'At the Monthly Meeting held for the particular Meeting of ffriends in Wensleydale at the house of Richard Robinson at Countersett the last day of the 11th moneth 1681'. Richard and his son Michael often dealt with the Meeting's finance and they managed several trusts which made regular payments to poor and needy Quakers. In times of distress or disaster special collections were made and two can be quoted, typical of many. In 1682, 16s. 10d. came in 'for the supply of ffriends necessities who have suffered for truths sake, in and about Bristoll and Gloster'. In 1704, £2 8s. 2d. was raised 'towards the Repairing the Damage Suffered by Tho: Thompson Sn: and Thomas Thompson Jun: by an Accident of fire'.

Instructions were issued in 1682 for the recording of all births, marriages and burials and the following year Richard was appointed recorder of the sufferings of Friends within the Wensleydale Meeting. One of his first entries was dated 3 January, 1683 and concerned his near neighbour Bartholomew Harrison who, 'having not been well', sent for Richard that he may write in his book a 'Testimony against his owne disorderly wayes . . . being subject to take a sup (as he called it) of drink & the letting his Tongue clatter to the dishonour of God'. Poor Bartholomew. Richard took it all down and it remains to this day, proof that early Quakers were human after all.[5]

All manner of interesting detail concerning Dales' life towards the end of the 17th century can be found in this minute book. In 1684 Friends paid 2s. 6d. rent for the stable they used in Bainbridge and in 1686 they paid 19s. 8d. for a new roof for the Meeting House, 13s. 4d. for '6 Cartfull of Ling & 5 Cartfull of seave thack' with 6s. 4d. to William Mason 'for thatching'. The following year they paid 1s. 5d. 'Hearth Money of the Meeting House'.

> 11th 3m 1687. Ordered . . . that the first day Meetings, when in Raydale Side be first at Richard Robinsons then at Carrend and so as formerly . . . Law: Routh acquainted this Meeting w[i]th his former and p[re]sent thoughts of Transporting himself and family into America.
>
> 6th 5m 1687. The Meeting considers building a Meeting House at Hawes but ffriends without Hawes quarter . . . are unwilling that one Meeting House for all be built in Hawes Quarter.
>
> 8th 6m 1688. Ed: Harrison and Michael Robinson is appointed to see ye Meeting House att Bainbridge to make alterations.[6]

The North Riding was rich in colourful characters and Philip Swale must rank as one of the most interesting. He was a Quaker and for much of his life he acted as agent for Philip Lord Wharton. It is perhaps misleading to single him out among the early Friends, many of whom were equally worthy of note, but by great good fortune we have access to a considerable amount of his business and personal correspondence and for that reason he emerges at the centre of his circle. His letters and papers are invaluable to historians of many interests and as several concern Richard Robinson they cannot be neglected here.[7]

Philip Swale came of the old Swaledale family of that name from Grinton and lived at Hartforth, north of Richmond. He was employed by the Whartons to manage their land and lead mines in Swaledale. He had a particular interest in lead mining, was an 'adventurer' in his own right, and was a party to a lease of the Swaledale mines with Lord Wharton. He also took a lease of lead mines at Kettlewell with his uncle Francis Smithson, and Robert Barker in 1670.[8]

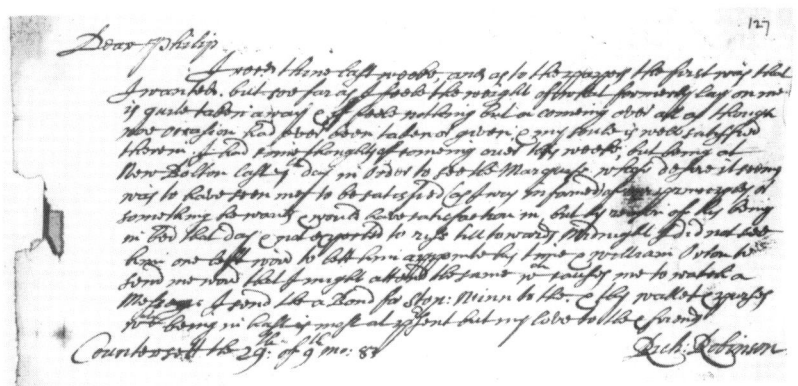

Dear Philip,

I rec[eive]d thine last weeke, and as to the papers the first was that I wanted. but soe far as I feele the weight of what formerly lay on me is quite taken away & I feele nothing but a comeing over all as though noe occasion had ever been taken or given & my soule is well satisfied therein. I had some thoughts of comeing over this weeke, but being at New Bolton last 7th day in Order to see the Marquess whose desire it seems was to have seen me to be satisfied (as I was informed) of our princeples or something he wants & would have satisfaction in, but by reason of his being in bed that day & not expected to riss till towards Midnight I did not see him one left word to lett him appointe his time & William Orton to send me word that I might attend the same w[hi]ch causes me to watch a Message. I send the a Bond for Step[hen] Winn to the & thy wallet & purses w[hi]ch being in hast is most at p[re]sent but my love to the & friends
Countersett the 29th of 9th Mo. [16]83

Rich[ard] Robinson.

Richard Robinson's letter to Philip Swale concerning his visit to Bolton Hall to explain 'our princeples' to the Marquess of Winchester. From Countersett, 29 November, 1683.

Richard Robinson's relationship with Philip Swale falls into three distinct categories – as a friend, as a Quaker and as a legal adviser. Indeed, the fact that Richard was able to offer advice concerning complicated legal matters has not yet been fully explained. That he and Philip Swale were on very familiar terms is beyond doubt. Richard wrote of Philip as 'a man well known unto many men of several Qualities, and of good Repute, being Servicable in his Generation' – but that was for public exhibition. Their personal correspondence was much more intimate. In 1681 Richard wrote of his heartfelt grief on hearing of the death of Philip's wife, and Philip concludes a reply with 'Thy affectionate friend Phil Swale'. A mutual friend, Thomas Rudd, wrote from Southwark Prison in 1684 'I shall be glad to hear from thee, [and] from Richard Robinson'. This is not altogether as surprising as it might seem when we discover that Thomas Rudd was a north-countryman himself, from Wharfe, near Austwick north of Settle. Other letters tell of Richard's varied activities including a proposed mission to Stockton and Yarm with work on 'Masham side' in 1683, and an expedition into Westmorland in 1688. A measure of the understanding between these two men and an insight into Richard's legal ability can be gleaned from two letters and a memorandum written in 1683. On 11 May Philip conveyed eight letters and two parchments to Richard for his perusal and opinion. These included and were mainly concerned with the 'Deed of Assignment' for Swale's interest in the Wharton lead mines. Philip asked for a reply 'as soon as thou can with conveniency' but Richard was 'under an excercise as to something upon my spirit soe that at this time I am not fitt for a concerne in such affaires', thus the advice he sent on 15 May relating to 'leadworkes' was not as comprehensive as the author would have wished.

John Chaytor of Richmond was another staunch Friend who occupied a prominent position in local affairs. His familiarity with the Sheriff of Richmond was to prove particularly valuable to Friends during the winter of 1683-4 when many were held in the House of Correction at Richmond. John Chaytor negotiated a complete discharge for them all but had to plead a postponement 'for friends coming in, in regard of the badness of the weather'. This incident highlights the situation peculiar to Friends of a person serving a prison sentence outside the prison. The Richmondshire Quakers finally assembled in John Chaytor's house and were formally dismissed by the Sheriff. John sent details to Philip Swale, 25 January, 1684 with a note that 'friends are now a goeing home Generally, Richard Robinson is prevailed withall to goe with Massam friends, I had noe minde he should goe for Wensleydale as judging it has ardous if not Impossable'.

Richard's involvement is not explained but it was probably connected with events in the following summer. On 14 June he was committed to the jail in Richmond again, and Philip, as a person of some influence in the town intervened on his behalf but to no avail. The somewhat trumped up charge stood and he was held for another three years.[9]

Philip Swale died in 1687 and his will carried his estate in trust to 'my loving and well beloved ffriends John Chaytor of Richmond, Mercer. Thomas Johnson of Richmond, Butcher. Richard Robinson & Michael Robinson his son both of Countersett, Yeomen'.[10] He gave to 'the youngest child of every of my said Trustees the sum of ten pounds Apeice' and Rachel Robinson received one such legacy from her father. The original receipt has survived among the Semerdale deeds and for all that Richard did not sign it he clearly wrote it and it remains, a good example of his small, neat, distinctive hand.

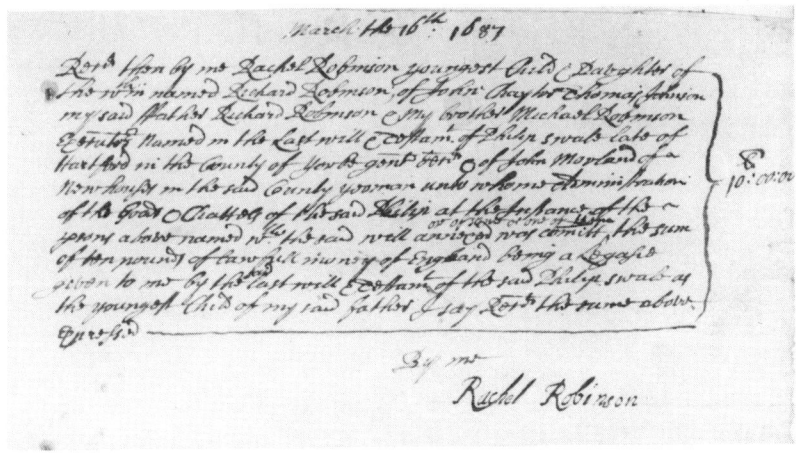

Rachel Robinson's receipt for Philip Swale's legacy, 16 March, 1687 [o.s.]

March the 16th: 1687. Rec'd then by me Rachel Robinson youngest Child & Daughter of the w[i]thin named Richard Robinson, of John Chaytor, Thomas Johnson, my said ffather Richard Robinson & My brother Michael Robinson Executors Named in the Last will & Testam[en]t of Philip Swale late of Hartford in the County of Yorke gent[leman] dec[ease]d & of John Morland of Newhouses in the said County Yeoman unto whome Administration of the Goods & Chattels of the said Philip at the Instance of the p[er]sons above named w[i]th the said will annexed was comitt or of some or one of them the sum of ten pounds of lawfull money of England being a Legasie given to me by the said last will & Testam[en]t of the said Philip Swale as the youngest Child of my said father I say Rec'd the sume above Expressed. By me Rachel Robinson.[11]

Early in the reign of William and Mary a much needed reform, the Act of Toleration, brought English dissenters freedom of belief and practice. One clause required the registration of meeting places and a list of those in Wensleydale was presented to the Court of Quarter Sessions at Thirsk on 8 October, 1689. Two were at Countersett, Richard Robinson's for one and the other no doubt 'the house of John ffothergill at Carrend' as minuted in 1682. There was one each at Bainbridge, Hawes, Carperby, West Burton, Carlton and Leyburn. Later others were licenced at Aysgarth in 1704, Chantry near West Witton in 1720, and Carlton in Coverdale in 1743.[12]

At last, after nearly half a century of persecution, the Quakers were free to worship as they pleased. Richard Robinson is counted among the 'Valiant Sixty' who had pioneered the cause but the years of hardship began to take their toll. His work declined, though not his fervour, and he rarely travelled far from home. As he retired his family came to the fore to take their places in the Society and in the community as a whole.

The year 1689 was an eventful one for them all. During the summer John Robinson was married and settled on the farm at Semerdale and in the autumn Richard's wife, Margaret, died at Countersett. What little we know about her leaves no doubt of her brave and able spirit. A note in a minute book shows her handling the Meetings' finance in Richard's absence and the following extract from a book of suffering came from her hand.

> ffriends, this is my Testimony for the truth against paym[en]t of Tithes, Steeplehouse Assessments and Clerks wages and all such like things, it is my faith and belief that they ought not by us (who profess the precious truth) to be paid, And for my part I pay none, though often (upon my husbands accompt) they have been demanded, neither do I ever intend to pay any, but through Gods assistante I hope to stand against them, and as concerning our Womens Meeting I will esteem of them, as being of good service to the Keeping of things in good order amon[g]st us. Margaret Robinson.[13]

The Robinson children described Richard's early struggles, 'And though at that time our Dear Mother had not joyned herselfe to friends . . . did she never Indeavor to hinder, but rather further him in those exercises'. She died at Countersett Hall, 1 November, 1689, and was buried at Bainbridge next day.[14] George Fox died two years later and Richard was so moved that he wrote a long appreciation of him and his ministry since the time that 'This messenger of the Lord came into our Parts in the third month, 1652 . . . and from that Day and Time I became affected to him . . . although there were but few that professed the Truth in these Parts'.[15] When Mary Robinson married John Hillary from Birk Rigg at John Robinson's house at Semerdale, 4 June, 1692, Richard was there and signed the marriage certificate along with 30 members of the assembled company.[16]

Richard continued 'very diligent' in his work but confided to a friend that he 'thought his time here was much over'. The premonition proved correct. During a First Day Meeting held at his house 31 December, 1693, 'he Bare a Living & Powerfull Testimony of the Lords appearance in that Meeting, to the admiration of the many good friends there p[re]sent, and in the Latter part of the Meeting, finding himself somewhat to decline, he desired to Lye down upon abedd, severall friends accompanying him there, where after he had lain still a while, departed this Life in much peace & Quietness, without the least appearance of pain'. Two days later his remains were taken down to Bainbridge, with 'many friends & others Accompanying him', to be buried at Holme Bray.[17]

Richard's five surviving children, with John Hillary and Elizabeth Robinson, drafted a Testimony from which most of the *First Publishers of Truth* account is drawn. Mary Hillary, Elizabeth Routh, John and Elizabeth Richardson, Mary Simson and Hannah Pratt all wrote individual Testimonies but that from Wensleydale Meeting carried 24 signatures. Richard Robinson was to them a 'Dear and Antient Friend and Brother'. They were:–

John Potts	James Metcalfe
Franc Thompson	Anthony Metcalfe
James Calvert	John Routh
John Binks	Thomas Routh
James Wetherald	John Routh
Wm Richardson	Richard Routh
Alex Stockdale	Richard Binks
John Stockdale	James Wetheralt
John Array	Christopher Routh
Alex Metcalfe	James Thompson
Alex Fothergill	William Metcalfe
Francis Metcalfe	Oswold Routh

Ten years after his death Richard Robinson was remembered as 'a man of a large Understanding, & was very Servicable in his Country upon divers accounts, & much beloved, being a good Example in Conversation', the first Quaker in Wensleydale.[18]

PART II

Later Generations

Faith and Prosperity

THE YEAR 1700 HAS BEEN SEEN as a watershed for Quakers. This is very evident in the lives of the second generation of Quaker Robinsons, Michael, John and Ephraim, the surviving sons of Richard and Margaret Robinson. Most of the 'Valiant Sixty' were dead and with them went much of the vigorous expansionism which had typified Friends in the early days. Where Richard had spent his time and energy across a wide field they confined themselves to home and farming and carved out for a certain prosperity and influence in the Dale. They applied their abilities with skill and honesty both within and outside the Society of Friends.

The brothers seem to have received individual portions of their father's property in their own hands before he died. Strangely, for a man of his understanding, Richard left no will, or if he did it has not survived. If he had already disposed of his land he may have thought the drafting of such a document of little urgency, and as we know, his end came rather quickly if not altogether unexpectedly. Had the law of primogeniture applied Michael as eldest son would have inherited all. This appears not to have been the case, a supposition born out by John's mortgage of Semerdale in his own right in 1711. Ephraim occupied Holly House farm and had confirmation of ownership in Michael's will in 1712. There is no description of Michael's holding but he had the lion's share, the family home at Countersett with responsibility for younger members of the family and much else beside.

The records of the Lord's Trustees of the Manor of Bainbridge show Michael and John Robinson joining the Trust, which their father had been so deeply involved in creating, when it changed hands for the first time in 1705. Their brother-in-law, John Hillary of Burtersett, joined at the same time.

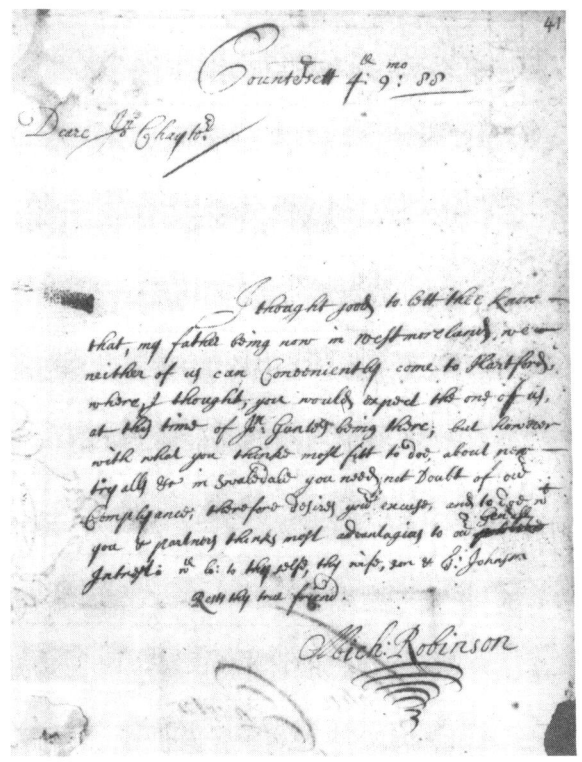

Countersett 4th 9mo [16]88

Deare Jo[h]n Chaytor.

    I thought good to lett thee know that, my father being now in Westmoreland we neither of us can Conveniently come to Hartford, where, I thought, you would expect the one of us, at this time of Jo[h]n Gunters being there, but however with what you thinke most fitt to doe, about new tryalls &c in Swaledale you need not Doubt of our Complyance, therefore desires your excuse, and to doe w[ha]t you & partners think most advantagias to our Gen[er]all Intrest. w[i]th lo[v]e to thyselfe, thy wife, son & T. Johnson.

                      Rests thy true friend.

                        Mich[ael] Robinson

Michael Robinson's letter to John Chaytor of Richmond, as a trustee of Philip Swale's estate, concerning new trials at the lead mines in Swaledale. From Countersett, 4 November, 1688.

Richard Robinson was deeply involved in the business side of lead mining whilst Philip Swale lived, and after his death as a trustee with Michael. His practical ability is demonstrated by the letter of 1688. It is not surprising therefore to find John Robinson taking a lease of lead mining ground with James Gorton, a miner from Low Row, in 1707.

Their 21 year lease allowed them to make trials and to mine for lead on Countersett Crag, Wether Fell, Dodd Fell and Cam Fell as far west as the County boundary. Small overgrown mine workings may be found all over the area but the mineral deposits were small so the smelt mill complex that they planned for Horton Gill, beside the Roman Road above Burtersett, was never built.[1]

Michael's house at Countersett remained the principal centre of activity for Wensleydale Quakers but change was at hand. In November 1696 they had bought an old building beside the Meeting House at Bainbridge and converted it into a Meeting House for the use of Quakers 'residing on or about Bainbridge and Raydaleside'. It came into use 5 October, 1697[2] and soon took over the role of Countersett Hall. The minute books show the Meeting in action and the problem it had with Edward Harrison who, though not an Elder, took to sitting in the ministers' gallery, an intolerable situation. Edward claimed that work he had done on the building entitled him to do so but Friends did not agree. They resolved that 'Ed: Harrison to refrain Sitting in the Gallery, and if he will not be persuaded, that some means be used to Restrain him'. The outcome is not known.

Quakers have always been literary minded people and those of Wensleydale were no exception. They maintained a small collection of books for borrowing from an early date and noted them in the minute book thus: 1682, 'James Stockdall had the Booke No Cross No Crown'. In time a set of rules regulating loans was issued with a directive 'That Such Books as belong this Meeting may be better preserved & do their Service more effectively 'tis agreed that they be all brought in to the house of Michael Robinson of Countersett and there be kept'.[3]

The brothers progressed and again, unlike their father, who was seldom out of trouble, they were comparatively law abiding. Michael had a brush with the law in 1684 when he and several companions were hauled before the magistrates at Richmond for 'unlawful assembly', that is meeting for worship illegally, in the house of James Ianson at Leyburn.[4] In January, 1697 he and John were prosecuted with several of their friends for chasing and destroying hares with greyhounds at Aysgarth the previous November.[5]

As the first decade of the 18th century drew on Michael Robinson conceived and completed a scheme to give Countersett Friends Meeting, which had functioned in his house for almost 60 years, a permanent

Countersett Friends Meeting House as completed in 1778 with the courtyard of 1781.

home. Therefore, 'About the year 1710 ... [he] ... built and appropriated'[6] a new Meeting House on the site of an old building in the middle of the village and incorporating some of its materials. It was largely rebuilt later but parts of Michael's building stand within the present Meeting House.

Michael Robinson died at Countersett 11 October, 1712 and was buried in the Friends Burial Ground at Bainbridge two days later. He had made a will on the first of the month, in the presence of his neighbours, James and Anthony Thwaite, which demonstrates a lively and benevolent interest in others of his family.

> One Gray hors[e] Called Page & one Bedstead & Beding thereunto belonging & one Silver Salt all which last mentioned I give unto my Sister Rachel, and likewise one Silver spoon w[hi]ch I give unto my Cousin Margaret Hillary, And I do hereby Nomenate Constitute & appoint My said Brother John Robinson my sole & absolute Executor of this my Last will & Testament Willing & Enjoyning him to take due Care of my Brother Emanuel to supply him with Meat drink Clothing & Lodging for & during his Naturall Life, And if att any time hereafter itt Please Allmighty god to Restore him his Reasonable understanding & that then he be mindfull to goe from my Brother John Then my Will is That my Sd Brother John shall pay or Cause to be paid unto my sd Brother Emanuel the Sum of Six pounds Yearly & every Year for and during his Natural Life for & Towards his support and Mentenance.

An inventory of goods and chattles was drawn up by James Metcalfe, John Hillary and George Metcalfe which shows Michael with a holding of live and dead stock to the value of £294 13s. 4d. He was a prosperous man for the Dales in 1712.[7]

Only very rarely is the death of a Friend noted in the minutes of Wensleydale Preparative Meeting but that happened in the case of Michael Robinson, 7 January, 1713 when the Meeting at Countersett decided that 'Forasmuch as our Esteemed friend Michael Robinson is lately deceased, who for Severall years, was A lawfull overseer and Elder in the Church amongst us, friends of this Meeting under A due and weighty Consideration of the Matter doe Generally Agree to Appoint (his Brother) Ephraim Robinson to Supply his place in the Said Office'.[8] A fitting close to the life of a second generation Friend.

Much that has been said of Michael applies equally well to Ephraim who was also a bachelor. He lived at the farm near Semerdale called Holly House where fragments of his house survive, though much altered after his day. His closes nearby can be easily identified. In 1712 they consisted of the fields called Goodeymidles with the dwelling house and barn on it, Willowmires, Renneson bottoms, Tonguehill, Nook with an outhouse, High Close, Low Close, Kettlewell Close and Braickenslack with an outhouse. These nine closes made a farm of about 30 acres of old enclosed land to which were attached five cattle gates on the Crag, five and a half in Bardale and five on Bainbridgeside, held under an ancient King's rent of 27s.[9]

Ephraim established himself at Holly House, no doubt with a servant or two, and extended hospitality generously much as his father had done at Countersett. An undated note of about 1710 preserved in Friends' archive directs that:

> The friends whose names are underwritten are to Accompany the Ministering friends that may come to visit our Meeting (each one by turn) to the next Meeting they travell to, when the Said friends do Lodge either at Bainbrigg or Countersett or the places adjacent.

James Wetherald, Senior	James Metcalfe
John Potts	Ephraim Robinson
Joseph Dobinson	John Robinson
James Scott or Edward	John Fothergill
John Ogden	Thomas Thompson or James
James Wetherald, Junior	Christopher Nicholson
Thomas Metcalfe	Thomas Lambert
Michael Robinson	James Calvert
George Metcalfe	James Blades[10]

A similar note dated 1709 concerned the horse not the man when James Wetherald was instructed 'to buy 6 bushell of oats for travelling friends horses, to be Lodged 2. Bushells at Hawes, 2 B. at Bainbridge and John Ogdens, and 2 B. at Countersett and Carrend'.[11] There is little more known of the life of Ephraim Robinson but he was clearly active in Meeting where his name crops up regularly. He served on several Trusts and in 1720 he supervised the repair of Bainbridge Meeting House. The following year he is noted in Quarter Sessions, the victim of robbery.[12] Later he appears to have left the farm at Holly House for he died at Bainbridge, 7 June, 1735, aged 72 years. He left no will and his property passed to his eldest surviving brother, John, whose sons, Richard and Amos drew up and published an inventory of his goods. They are typically the odds and ends of a retired farmer but include a good mare valued at £5 and 'a Little parcell of Hay'.[13]

Of the nine children born to Richard and Margaret Robinson at Countersett John alone left Robinson heirs. John Robinson was a man of enormous influence in the Dale, second only to his father in that respect, and exceptional among the Robinsons in that he lived to a ripe old age. He was born at Countersett, 12 January, 1658 and lived, so far as is known, in or near that village all his life. He married Elizabeth Smith from Sowerby near Halifax at Abraham Hodgson's house in Halifax, 26 June, 1689. John and Elizabeth settled at Semerdale House, half a mile north east of Countersett on the Bainbridge road, and raised a family of ample proportions. Margaret was born in 1690, Susanna 1692, Richard 1694, Amos 1697, Benjamin 1698, John 1701, Elizabeth 1706, Abel 1710, and Joshua 1712. Abel, Susanna and Benjamin all died unmarried respectively in 1731, 1772 and 1784. Margaret cannot be traced. Elizabeth married William Blakey from Lea Yeat in Kirkby Malham parish, at Countersett Meeting House in 1733. Their descendants survived in Wensleydale to this century. The four sons, Richard, Amos, John and Joshua all lived long and useful lives in the Dale and we will meet them later.[14]

John, father of Richard and Amos, mortgaged his farm at 'Semerdale Nigh Countersett' to his brother-in-law John Hillary of Burtersett for £300, 8 January, 1711. John was resident and described the farm as:

> his Estate now Called & Known by the Name of Semerdale (That is to say) All that p[ar]cell of ground formerly being in one Close then Called west high semerdale but now divided into three Closes Called by the Names of west high semerdale, Parrack & Nurscerry with a Dwelling-house, stable, Peat house with severall other Nessecery houses Erected therin & a garding adjoining upon the East of the s[ai]d houses & a Court & fould before the door, and one Close of ground Called Midle semerdale with a laine between them containing all-together by Estemation Elleaven acres of ground . . .

The old wooden staircase at Countersett Hall with stout turned balusters under a strong banister rail. The staircase, with pine panelling and hams have disappeared.

& one other close called litle high semerdale & one other close called Cornclose now divided & called high corne Close & low corn Close with a Barn or feild house in the lower of them & one other close called litle mires all the last named Closes Containing by Estemacion Thirteen acres & a halfe of ground . . . and four Cattlegates in the pasture Called Countersett Cragg Together with all woods . . . Yielding and paying therefore Yearly & every Year forever hereafter unto our Soveraigne Lady the Queen . . . the Yearly Rent of Twenty three shillings & sixpence of Lawfull Money of Greatbritain.

The mortgage was intended to run for seven years but interest continued to be paid long after that and it was not redeemed until 1731 when Amos Robinson paid off Isaac and Mary Hillary as heirs of the original mortgagee.[15]

The death of Michael Robinson in 1712 brought to John virtually the whole of their father's estate and he probably moved to Countersett Hall. He is not described as of Semerdale after 1712 and much of the woodwork, panelling and glass at Countersett Hall suggest an extensive remodelling of the house early in the 18th century. John was certainly living at the family's home farm in 1715 when there is the first hint of a rift with his neighbour James Metcalfe concerning rights of way and the state of a field wall. It was noted in Monthly Meeting minutes in 1715 and again in 1717 when John drafted a letter thus:

The letter John Robinson wrote about his 'difference' with James Metcalfe over a right of way and the repair of drystone walls, 6 November, 1717.

> I do hereby Consent & agree that my son Richard shall & may Reffer the difference between James Metcalfe & me Touching the sufficiency of my Way by his Door &c The repair of Mark faw wall deviding from my Haws, & the Tresspases done me by its Insuffitiency, And in case the Arbetrat[or]s do make an End will stand to it p[ro]vided James oblige himselfe to do the like= as Witness my hand. Jo[h]n Robinson. The 6th 9thMo 1717.

Four Friends were appointed to deal with this and delivered their verdict to both parties and to the Meeting. John accepted their decision but James did not and the matter rumbled on and came before Preparative Meeting 18 years later. To have refused a directive from such a quarter is unusual, but John Robinson was not the only one to suffer from James Metcalfe's wrath. In the minute of 5th 2m 1738:

> George Metcalfe hath this day made a complaint against his Ounkel James Metcalfe for endevouring to throw upon him more rent than appears to belong to him, likewise in Cutting of his wood at fow futt beside Semerwater Side & some other things.[16]

Among John Robinson's many undertakings for the Society of Friends was the administration of the 'hors silver', a Trust founded by Philip Swale with £5 left to provide a horse for a woman Friend without one of her own thereby enabling her to attend Monthly Meeting. In 1732 John gave 6s. 6d. from 'the Hors silver to his sister Rachel to be laid out by the Women for Margt Verity'. And in 1738 he conveyed the entire Trust, which was by then worth £8, by deed to his sister Rachel Robinson. The shedding of responsibility continued with a note to the Meeting that:

> John Robinson grown old desired to have his accounts Inspected relating to the poor so friends appoints Joseph Dobinson & Alex: Fothergill to go to John's house at some suitable time and make report to next Meeting.

This they duly did and returned a satisfactory answer.[17]

At the age of 82 John died, at Countersett, 4 July, 1739. He had made his will the previous December and divided his property among his four sons. Richard as the eldest acted as executor and chief beneficiary, made provision for his widow, Elizabeth, who was to have £8 a year and 'free houseroom in my now dwelling house or some convenient part of it so long as she may be mindfull to remain in it and also to have the Bed we used to Layin'. Similar arrangements were also made for dependent members of the family, Benjamin and Susanna, with each claim tied to property. The Blakey grandchildren were in receipt of small legacies.[18] Elizabeth Robinson lived on at Countersett and died there 27 January, 1742.

The Last of the Yeomen

Four men, Richard, Amos, John and Joshua, the sons of John and Elizabeth Robinson of Semerdale, dominate the history of the Robinson family throughout most of the 18th century. Richard and John remained bachelors at Countersett, Amos married and raised a family at Semerdale, and Joshua though he married, left no heir. We first notice Richard, the eldest, at the age of 16, signing the Semerdale mortgage deed in 1711 with his uncles Michael and Ephraim.[1] He was also present when their father released the Thistlepot-Borwins lands to Amos in 1727. Amos was soon to be married and John:

> in Consideration of the Paternall Love & affection which I have and bear unto my Second Son Amos Robinson for his filiall part & Childs portion and Towards his support & mentenance as also for & in Consideration of his undertaking the payment & discharge of severall sums of money which I am owing unto severall persons according to a schedull delivered to him in writing Hath Given & Granted and by these presents Doth Give Grant & Confirm unto my said son Amos . . . All that field or pasture ground Called & Known by the name of Ingheads & one Close of ground Called Souterkeld about four acres . . . & one other Close of Ground Called forty pence & one Close of ground Called pryclose & one . . . close of ground Called Thistlepot which thre last mentioned Closes Contain by Esteemation about nine acres . . . and other two Closes of meadow ground Called Borwinses Containing by Esteemation six acres . . . & one other Close of Meadow ground Called great Myers Containing by Esteemation four acres . . . also the Right of Redemption of all that Measuage & Tenement Called & Known by the name of Semerdale,

with four cattlegates on Countersett Crag, eight in Bardale Pasture, and ten on Bainbridgeside Pasture, all in the possession of Amos Robinson under the ancient fee farm rent of £2 8s. 5d., together with common rights of pasture and turbary, etc.[2]

The marriage of Amos Robinson and Ann Metcalfe took place at Bainbridge Friends Meeting House in 1729 but their union was short lived for Ann soon died. Amos lived on at Semerdale and negotiated its redemption from mortgage with John Hillary's widow and son in 1731. He also had confirmation from his father of his right to Semerdale in 1738 and to the Thistlepot Borwins lands in 1739. This last also brought him 'an Equall undivided part and Share of the Royalties of the Lordship & Mannor of Bainbridge . . . proportionable to my said Son Amos Robinson's frehold Estate at Semerdale as well as of the Lands & premises hereby given . . . according to the . . . Lease & Release granted and Conveyed to me and other freeholders for a competent Sum of money in hand paid to one Anthony Fothergill survivor of the first purchasers' of the said royalties.[3]

The death of John the father in 1739 brought about the complete fragmentation of the property. Amos, being already in receipt of a generous portion, received nothing beyond 'a Competent Share of my Law=Books'. John had Verity House and the Cragend land and Joshua had Holly House farm. The residue of 'Messuages, Lands & Tenements & Cattlegates . . . personal Estate, Goods, Chatles, debts, rights & Credits . . .' passed to Richard as sole executor.[4] The exact size of this portion is unknown but it was extensive and included the house and farm at Countersett and the 67 acre Countersett West Pasture. Richard sold the West Pasture in 1740 to his brother-in-law William Blakey who was already 'erecting a building or new Dwelling house'. It was called Thorns House, now derelict, near Woodend.[5] In 1756 Richard Robinson purchased a ruined cottage and two garths near the Meeting House at Countersett and added them to his home farm.[6]

John's Verity House cannot now be identified but it was described in 1739 as a dwelling house 'with an additionall part Consisting of two litle Rooms adjoining on the south side thereof & one garth Called low garth on the south side of the said house and one other parcell of ground Called per adjoining upon the parrack & hargill with free Ingress Egress & regress to the said dwelling house on both sides thereof as now used'.[7] Bearing in mind the problem of a right of way, the right of access stress, the position of the Per, and the fact that John reinforced the access question in 1777, it appears likely that Verity House stood on the site of the barn between the Meeting House and Low House Farm. John also had the Cragend lands which consisted of three closes and one other called West Close to the east of them.

The bachelor brothers Richard and John Robinson stayed on at the family farm at Countersett Hall, or whatever name they used for it. 'Hall' appears to be a modern innovation. With them lived their sister Susanna, brother Benjamin and a servant or two including Eleanor Proctor as housekeeper and Simon Thwaite as a general servant. The situation of Reuben Harrison is by no means clear but he occupied New Close House, now almost certainly Boar Inn and was probably the hind or farm servant. Later, from about 1790, when all the brothers had died he occupied Countersett Hall farm as tenant in his own right.

Joshua Robinson inherited his uncle Ephraim's farm at Holly House in 1739 and undertook a massive remodelling. The work was carried out with considerable style and the house remains much as Joshua made it with handsome stone architraves, as at Carr End, and an unmoulded stone doorway with a cornice and a keystone engraved 'Jo[a] Robinson, 1740.' Here he set up house and had himself described as a yeoman of Hollinghouse when, in 1754, he married Elizabeth Hoyle of Burnley at Marsden Meeting House.

Holly House date stone showing Joshua Robinson's initials and the date 1740.

Amos Robinson married Jane Pratt of Hollinghouse as his second wife, at Countersett Meeting House 9 March, 1747. They had four children, Elizabeth born in 1749, John 1750, Richard 1751 and Hannah 1753. Elizabeth and Richard died as infants.

Amos assumed something of his father's position among Friends and was active in their interests both spiritual and financial. In 1733 he supervised repairs at Bainbridge Meeting House and in 1735 did similar work at Hawes. He helped to manage various Trusts including the valuable 'Smithson' lands at Carperby which benefitted poor and needy Quakers in Richmond Monthly Meeting.[8] Alexander Fothergill mentions his mediation with Amos Robinson in a dispute between Thomas Metcalfe and William Blakey but gives no details of the contention.[9] Samuel Fothergill was much more forthcoming. As he travelled through Westmorland on a preaching tour in 1740, he wrote to his wife from James Wilson's house near Sedbergh on 21 May: 'I am favoured with a very agreeable companion this week, but I fear I cannot have his company forward. It is Amos Robinson, father's late companion to London. We have had Meetings appointed for every day except 7th day.'[10]

We will probably never know what prompted Amos Robinson to follow his grandfather's footsteps to the south but we can find confirmation of his visit in the minutes of London Morning Meeting, 4 February, 1739 to which he and John Fothergill, and others from Yorkshire, came with credentials thus:

> John Fothergill being on a Visit to Friends produced a Certificate from Knaresborough Monthly Meeting in Yorkshire dated the 20th day 10mo 1739, Signifying that he is in true Unity with them & that his Service both in the Ministry of the Gospel & the Discipline of the Church are well Received and Valued by them. Amos Robinson also his Companion produced a Certificate from the Monthly Meeting of Richmond in Yorkshire dated the 7th 10mo 1739, Signifying that he

was a Sober and Religiously minded Man, Carefull & Circumspect in his Conduct & Conversation & that they had Unity with him in his Intended Journey.

John Fothergill kept an account of his journey to and from London but at no stage mentions his companions.[11]

Richard and Joshua Robinson were involved in a major reorganisation of the Wensleydale trust properties in 1756 and helped to draft a new Declaration of Uses for them. The deed stipulates that:

> forty or fifty pounds shall be paid or Offered to be paid towards the purchasing or Building A Meeting House . . . at Redmire, West Witton or Swinithwaite . . . the Meetinghous at Bainbridge shall be floored with Boards and half the seats well Backt And the Remainder if any be [used] as it may seem to them to be most service Either to the said people called Quakers, or helping to mend or make Bridges at the lowend of Semerwater or the Isles in Swaledale.[12]

Richard supervised an extensive repair of Aysgarth Meeting House in 1760 and all the family suffered the ravages of distrainment for non-payment of tithes. The Quakers denied the right of anyone to levy tithes, a tenth was originally intended to support the parish clergy, much of which, by 1700 had passed into private hands. Quakers flatly refused to pay and so had their goods siezed quite legally by those entitled to the tithe of their lands. Farmers usually lost livestock, cheese or bacon but other goods such as stockings, firkins of butter, a pair of shoes or wool cards were taken, in upper Wensleydale, and auctioned at either Bainbridge or Askrigg.

The Robinsons were distrained upon every year and the practice assumed a ritual order in which they always lost, for if the goods in auction failed to make the tithe value the deficiency was added to the next year's assessment.

Year	Name	Amount	Type	Loss	Sold for
1756	Amos Robinson	for £2.13.9.	Tythes etc:	lost one young Heifer	sold for £2.10.0.
	Richard Robinson	for 6.6.	Tythes etc:	lost Cheese	sold for 9.
	John Robinson	for 1. 9.4½.	Tythes etc:	lost One Heifer	sold for 2.13.0.
1761	Amos Robinson	for 1. 1.0.	Tythes etc:	lost A Ham of Bacon & Ham	sold for 1. 0.7.
	Joshua Robinson	for 12.0.	Tythes etc:	lost Six Stone of Cheese	sold for 6.8.
	Richard Robinson	for 10.8.	Tythes etc:	lost A Ham of Bacon	sold for 2.6.
	John Robinson	for 12.6.	Tythes etc:	lost Wool and Cheese	sold for 2.9.

The record of a sale at Askrigg in April 1766 shows Amos Robinson's loss in great detail. £1 0s. 7d. for tythe, 6s. 8d. Costs, 2s. 6d. Distress, 9d. Arrears gives a total of £1 10s. 6d. for which he lost hams worth £1 2s. 2d.[13] The Robinsons never paid tithes but they could not rid themselves of their legal obligation to pay them. Both Countersett Hall and Semerdale were still paying as recently as 1958.

The distrainment books show the Robinsons among their Quaker friends and neighbours and the Land Tax returns reveal their position throughout Wensleydale. Raydaleside had the largest concentration of Quakers in any part of the Dale, about one in four inhabitants being Friends. In Countersett it was almost total, with the Fothergill, Robinson, Blakey and Thwaite families all Quaker and at least one family of Metcalfes. The earliest surviving Land Tax return demonstrates the point in 1759.[14]

Alex: Fothergill	£2. 0. 0.	William Blakey	£1. 0. 0.
Ann Smith	3. 4.	Robert Tomlinson	6. 0.
Mary Pratt	1. 0. 0.	Reuben Metcalfe	11. 4.
Richard Robinson	1. 9. 0.	Ann Thwaite, widow	7. 8.
Amos Robinson	1. 7. 0.	James Thwaite	12. 0.
John Robinson	10. 0.	Francis Metcalfe	2. 6.
Joshua Robinson	14. 8.	John Metcalfe	5. 0.

One of the most unfortunate aspects of this account of Quaker yeomen is the absence of family papers hence the constant resort to legal documents and wills. This cannot but give a one-sided view, without the detail of everyday life. As the 18th century proceeded, so the Robinson brothers approached the end of their lives. On 11 January, 1765 Richard, 'being somewhat out of health in body, but of good Sound and perfect Disposing mind and Memory' drafted his will. Amos was appointed sole executor and his son John, then aged 15 years, the chief beneficiary. This was indeed inevitable. As the sole male Robinson heir, he would inherit the bulk of the family estate. Richard left property to his brothers but with reversion to John in every case. Provision was made for John's children, Susanna and Benjamin, and Amos' daughter Hannah was to have £500. A host of friends and relations had small legacies with three of Reuben Harrison's children Daniel, Elizabeth and Alice, having one guinea each and the youngest, Margaret, two guineas. £100 was to be invested and the interest applied to a Quaker schoolmaster:

> within the Wensleydale particular Meeting and within the Constablery of Bainbridge . . . Also I give Ten pounds Towards the Building of a good Stone Arched Bridge at the foot of Semerwater Provided that it be built and Completed within five Years after my Decease.[15]

In less than a month Richard was dead and buried at Bainbridge 2 February, 1765 aged 71 years. If we seek a memorial for him we could take it to be the handsome stone bridge near Semerwater which, as we have seen, Quakers were considering building as early as 1756. The five year proviso was adhered to and a fragment of account survives in the Quakers' Archive.

Semerwater bridge as built by Quaker initiative about 1770 and restored by the North Riding Quarter Sessions in 1874.

Semerwater Bridge.

	£. s. d.
Cash paid to workmen and for materials for building the said Bridge. (Besides work done by the neighbours in filling up the ends & making the road over, worth £10 more.)	90. 1. 1.
Money given and collected towards building the Bridge omounts only to	60. 14. 0.
The Undertakers & Managers (Besides all their time, trouble & attendance) are out of pocket	30. 7. 1.

In the following hands;

	£. s. d.	
Amos Robinson	4. 0. 0.	
Joshua Robinson	4. 0. 6.	
John Robinson	1. 4. 9.	
John Thwaite	7. 2. 3.	
Alexander Fothergill	12. 18. 7.	
John Outhett	10. 6.	
Thomas Lambert, Snr.	10. 6.	30. 7. 1.

We therefore desire your Cheerfull and generous contribution to make up the said defficiencie and enable us to repair the damage done to it by some great Floods etc.[16]

The bridge remains much as they made it, though extensively repaired by the County in 1874. In style it is typically 18th century, a worthy memorial to the Quaker yeomen. Richard's bequest to a Quaker school also acted as a spur to serious activity and Alexander Fothergill generously gave a site for it in the middle of Countersett near the Meeting House. At a Meeting at Countersett, 6 January 1768, Friends decided that:

> The Building of a Stable for the Use & Acommodation of friends horses at Countersett being Under fr[ien]ds Consideration the following persons Are Appointed to consider & make Calculation as Near as they can. What Sum of Money May be Nesesary for the finishing the Same & Likewise to make an agreement with Som, Suitable persons to get Matterials & lay them at the place (Viz) Alex. Fothergill, Amos Robinson, John Thwaite, John Robinson, John Wetherald, and Thomas Lambert Jun.[17]

The following year, 1769, Friends note that 'a Stable for the Use of Friends horses and a Schoolhouse Over it which is intended to be Builded upon a peece of Ground Belonging to Alexander Fothergill.'[18] There was a snag however when it was discovered that the property was under mortgage. But, once the agreement of the mortgagee had been secured on payment of 10s. in 1772, work went ahead.[19] A schoolroom was built with a stable for visiting Friends under it, and a schoolmaster employed, a situation highly beneficial for Raydaleside Friends and one which was extended to non-members.

On 4 April, 1767 the Manor of Bainbridge was conveyed to new trustees for a third time.[20] Amos and John Robinson joined the Trust on the strength of their freehold. Amos expanded his in 1770 when he bought from Reuben Metcalfe, the two closes which separated the Countersett Hall and Semerdale land. These were Borwins Close, four acres with 'one out House or Barn standing in the High end thereof' and Kettlewell Close, four acres, 'adjoining the North corner of the said Borwins' with 1½ cattle gates on the Crag and 1½ cattle gates on Bainbridgeside. The price was £252.[21]

Amos Robinson died in May, 1775 and left almost everything to his son John. His wife Jane was to have £20 a year for life and houseroom 'in this my Dwelling House or some other suitable place provided for her' as long as she remained unmarried. She was also to have 'that Half Dozen Silver Table Spoons Marked A.I.R.'. Hannah was to receive £500 and the 'Silver Pint that was brother Richard's After the decease of my Brother John (he being to have the use thereof during his life)'.[22]

Joshua Robinson of Holly House died four months after Amos and left his farm to his wife Elizabeth for life and then to his nephew Joshua Blakey.[23] Elizabeth Robinson lived on at Holly House and made a number of extended preaching tours, to America and around various parts of Britain, including Essex. We may thereby conjecture a meeting with George Gibson of Saffron Walden whom she married as his second wife at Countersett Meeting House in 1778.[24]

John Robinson lived out his life at Countersett Hall and died there 11 February, 1777. He left the bulk of his estate, including Verity House, to his nephew John Robinson. Like Richard, he left a host of small legacies to friends and relations with the interest on £50 to the Quaker schoolmaster.[25]

With the day of the Robinsons as residents of Countersett rapidly drawing to a close the records dwindle. After 1777 only the aged Benjamin survived from John's family at Semerdale, and he was mentally deficient. It appears that Amos's widow Jane Robinson and her daughter moved into Countersett Hall and perhaps kept the family together there with the help of the Harrisons who lived nearby.[26] Certainly Hannah was living at Countersett when she married at Countersett Meeting House, William Fothergill, the son of Alexander of Carr End, 14 August, 1782. Benjamin Robinson died at Countersett in 1784 and Jane Robinson at Carr End, 4 March, 1794, aged 81 years,[27] the last of the Robinsons as Quaker yeomen of Countersett Hall.

Conviction Fades and is Lost

From this point on the story of the Robinson family takes a very different course because John, the only surviving son of Amos and Jane, abandoned the Dales and became a professional man. We know little of John Robinson's early life other than that he was born at Semerdale 6 July, 1750 and received an education which fitted him for a career in medicine. He did not attend the school at Sedbergh as Doctors Hillary and Fothergill had done, but perhaps like them, he took an apothecary's apprenticeship, probably at Bradford. The careers of the two famous physicians would be well known to him being near neighbours in Wensleydale and William Hillary was first cousin to his father.[1] The background to John Robinson's medical career is to be found in Bradford, a town with a Friends Meeting, which in the mid-18th century became 'rich in apothecaries and doctors'.[2]

In 1741 the 27 year old apothecary, Joshua Walker of Sundial House, bought a small estate in Bowling and built a substantial home which he named Upper House. It still stands, beside the road from Bradford to Wakefield, a little way from Bradford city centre, built from the pleasant biscuit coloured sandstone which is used so generously in quoins, strings, jambs, sills, lintels and a moulded cornice. It has a large double-pile block under a hipped roof and gabled wings at either end. Formerly the whole area had a pleasant rural atmosphere,[3] with a circular sweep of gravel in front of the house and 'gardens, plantations and pleasure grounds' nearby as well as six closes of meadow called The Half Acre, Lane Close, Outnook, Ing, Croft, and Cow Close, Alas, all but the house have vanished under the sprawling mass of Bradford City and it is difficult to recognise the area to which Joshua Walker brought his newly wedded wife Margaret Waddington in 1743. Their first child, Elizabeth was born at Upper House in 1744 and it was she who married John Robinson of Semerdale at Bradford Friends Meeting House, 1 June, 1774.[4]

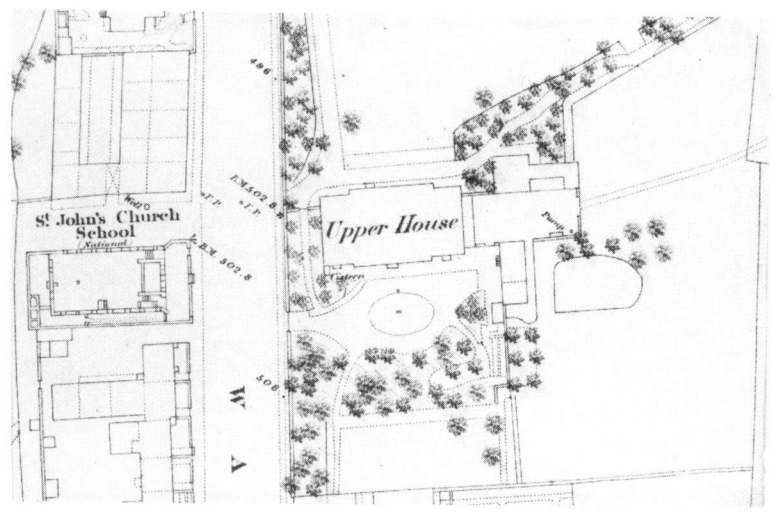

Plan of the Upper House area of Bowling, Bradford, the home of the Robinson family from 1778 to 1811.

John and Elizabeth Robinson returned to Semerdale for a time though it is not clear whether Amos and Jane still lived there. Certainly Amos's will of 1775 describes him as of Semerdale but his burial a few months later recorded him at Countersett. At any rate 'Semerdale Hall' was the home of John and Elizabeth Robinson when their eldest children, Margaret in 1775 and Richard in 1776, were born. Whilst at Semerdale they attended the Meeting House at Countersett and were present and signed the marriage certificate for Richard Thistlethwaite and Agnes Hunter on 8 May, 1776. Jane and Hannah Robinson, mother and sister of John, were also present.[5]

John Robinson owned the Meeting House having inherited it from his father Amos by way of his uncle Richard and grandfather John, the brother of Michael Robinson who built it. The Quakers had maintained it for many years and it was decided that they should have the freehold and this was duly conveyed to trustees 18 January, 1778.[6] John also relinquished his clerkship of Richmond Monthly Meeting[7] and by April 1778 had leased the farm at Semerdale for seven years to Jonathan Shaw.[8] The Robinsons packed up and left for Bradford.

They moved in with the Walkers at Upper House and three more children were born to them there: John in 1778, Jane Beatrix 1780, and Elizabeth Isabella 1782. Richard and Elizabeth Isabella died young. In the Friends' registers of births John the father is described as a yeoman[9] but a deed of 1791 shows him as an apothecary[10] and in a Directory of 1792 he is a surgeon.[11] Holdens' Bradford Directory for 1809-11 enters him as 'Robinson, John, surgeon, Upper House, Bradford'.[12] The Walkers died at Upper House, Margaret in 1792 and the aged Joshua in 1801.[13] Prior to that date Elizabeth Robinson enjoyed the Bowling estate from her father by gift and John Robinson bought the adjoining meadows called Gallow Close and Gallow Hirst in 1792.[14] In 1806 he recovered Holly House which his uncle had left to Joshua Blakey. The negotiations were long and complicated owing to the life interest of Elizabeth Gibson but after her death in 1804 John Blakey, the son of Joshua, released the farm to John so that a Robinson was once again in possesion of the entire family estate at Countersett.[15]

Elizabeth Robinson died in Bradford and was buried there 27 October, 1810, aged 66 years. John made his will 30 November, 1810, added a codicil 1 January, 1811, and died the next day, aged 61 years. He too, was buried in Bradford. John Robinson, Junior, had received the Bowling estate from his mother, and on the death of his father, inherited the Raydaleside lands. His sister Margaret, the wife of Sharp Roberts, and their daughter Elizabeth were all beneficiaries. So too was Jane Beatrix, who had married Thomas Saunderson from Hull. Thomas Saunderson and John Fothergill of Rochdale, the son of William and Hannah Fothergill of Carr End, were appointed executors. One clause may, under favourable circumstances, throw light on John Robinson's literary possibilities when he stated that to John and Beatrix 'I give and bequeath my Table Linen, Bed Linen, china and Books except the English Encyclopedia and my Manuscript Books'.[16] Unfortunately he left no instruction concerning the exempt items but they may still exist, though an extensive search has not found them.

Upper House was offered for sale almost at once.[17] It was not sold, but the Robinsons appear never to have lived there again. John Robinson, Junior, and his wife Mary, of whom we have no record, not even the details of a marriage, returned to the Dales and took up residence at Holly House for a year or two. It is difficult to understand why they did not move into Semerdale unless it was that they were having the house rebuilt.

Their first two children, Joshua Walker and Elizabeth, were born at Holly House in 1810 and 1812 but the next one, Mary, was born at Semerdale House in 1813 as were Helen in 1815 and Charlotte in 1816. Again mystery envelopes the story for Mary Robinson disappears from the records and the family returned to Bradford. John the father came back to marry Margaret, the daughter of the hosier James Burton Wood at Askrigg Church, 15 March, 1820.[18]

John and Margaret Robinson occupied a house somewhere near Bradford called Mount Pleasant for about four years and then one at Calverley, called Calverley Lodge, for three. Whilst there, in 1827, John sold the Upper House estate to several parties in lots. In 1828 the family moved into Eccleshill Hall, the early 18th century home of the Stanhopes, for which they paid 10 guineas a year furnished. Several children were born to John and Margaret over the years but as there is no consecutive record of them we cannot be certain of their number. Some were baptised at the parish church whilst others appear in birth notes from Brighouse Monthly Meeting. Five sons survived, namely, John, Richard, Henry Wood, Jeffery Wood and Amos. Of John's first family two at least survived: Elizabeth who married Greenwood Bentley, Junior, Solicitor of Bradford and Charlotte the wife of John Wood, Slate Merchant of Askrigg.

There is no hint that John Robinson (born 1778) ever had a profession. In 1820 he was an Esquire, in 1824 a Yeoman but thereafter solely a Gentleman and one, to judge from the number of times he mortgaged his property, familiar with that method of raising capital.[19]

In 1837 the family was still living at Eccleshill Hall, but not for long. In 1839 they moved to Kingston upon Hull for about three years, possibly longer. By 1845 they were back at Semerdale House where John Robinson died, 10 March, 1853. Margaret survived him by a mere two months. The estate, with the exception of Semerdale, which was secured to Margaret and her heirs by Settlement, passed to trustees who, on finding it heavily mortgaged, decided to sell. Thus Holly House, Countersett Hall, Cooper Mire and Crag Ends were duly conveyed to William Pilkington of the Grange, Wilpshire, near Blackburn, 26 November, 1853 for £6,400.[20]

Semerdale alone remained with the Robinsons, the owners being the five sons of John and Margaret as heirs of their mother. John, the eldest, born in Bradford in 1821, was a Surgeon who qualified in 1846 as M.R.C.S.[21] He practiced at one time in Goole but was in residence at Semerdale House by 1857. Gradually he bought his brothers' portions of the farm for £570 each. Jeffery Wood Robinson, 'late of Semerdale House', had become a miner at Sandhurst in the Colony of Victoria, Australia; Henry Wood Robinson was a 'Brewer and Spirit Merchant' at Askrigg and Amos Robinson was a Gentleman of Semerdale House. The remaining portion, that of Richard Robinson, could not be bought as Richard was 'Dumb' and had a capital trust created on his share.[22]

John Robinson settled into the 'Mansion House' at Semerdale with a hind or farm bailiff in Holly House to look after the 95 acre farm where he built up a considerable amount of 'valuable farm stock and implements of husbandry'.[23] In 1861 John Robinson was described as a retired Surgeon, Surgeon to the Volunteers, Landed Proprietor and Farmer. He employed two maids, a carter and an under groom at Semerdale with George Preston as hind or bailiff in Holly House.[24] The topographer J. J. Sheahan saw Semerdale about this time and described it as:

> Semerdale House, the seat of John Robinson Esq., . . . a handsome modern structure, erected on the site of an ancient mansion. The principal rooms are spacious and lofty, and the whole is finished and furnished with great taste and elegance. Adjoining it is a conservatory. The house stands in a fine elevated situation, commanding views of the most interesting scenery.[25]

Sadly, John Robinson fell into debt and decided to sell. A detailed and illustrated sale catalogue was prepared for the auction to be held at the Kings Arms Hotel, Askrigg, on 14 July, 1862. The sale was successful, therefore, on 29 December, 1862, John and his wife Ann Elizabeth Robinson of Thornesfield House, Thorne near Wakefield, set their hands to the conveyance that took Semerdale to William Pilkington for £3,500.[26] Thereby was severed the Robinsons' link with Countersett which had endured through two hundred and twelve years and six generations of that family.

Postcript

What then became of the Robinsons? John and Ann Elizabeth were but temporary residents at Thornesfield House. They moved on, perhaps to America, where the son of 'Mr. Robinson of Summerdale Hall' had been noted 'a Physician' in 1845. Richard, the second son, lived out his life unmarried, with Thomas and Elizabeth Middlemiss at Stalling Busk. He died there and was buried among Friends at Bainbridge in 1867, aged 43.

Henry took over the brewery which his uncle, James Burton Wood had at Askrigg. He went on to become a miner in Australia. Jeffery was at Semerdale when he mortgaged his share in that estate for £270 in April 1853, possibly to finance his emigration to Australia. Perhaps the brothers travelled out together for they both settled in the gold mining district of Sandhurst, now Bendigo, in Victoria. Jeffery is not heard of after May 1857 but Henry returned briefly to England later that year and helped settle up the Semerdale estate. Amos was still at Semerdale, a Gentleman, in April 1858 but is heard of no more. Perhaps he too joined his brothers in Australia leaving only John and Richard in England.

Henry was married in 1854, in Australia, and raised nine children. The eldest, born in 1855, was christened Henry Semerdale Robinson. The family left Sandhurst for Costerfield, also in Victoria, where Henry became a bricklayer and his elder sons had a gold mine called Robinsons Reef. Henry died in 1899 but his family stayed around Costerfield until the mines were exhausted.

One son, Richard Amos, moved to Boulder, Western Australia, in 1906. The remainder went to Melbourne. Costerfield is a mining ghost town now but the original Robinson family homestead survives. Henry's grand-daughter, Margaret Rigoll, visited it in 1979 and wrote, 'the old home which was originally a dozen rooms, but now reduced to eight . . . still stands . . . in disrepair and not habitable. The four huge quince trees were laden with fruit and the wisteria in bloom was climbing over the door at the entrance'.[27]

PART III

Stones and Mortar

Countersett Hall

ONE OF THE PRINCIPAL JOYS of a study such as this is the opportunity to discover and examine those places where the people most concerned lived and worked. The physical context helps to evoke the personalities being studied. Here we look closely at the houses where the Robinsons lived: Countersett Hall, Semerdale Hall, Holly House, the Boar Inn at Countersett, and the Meeting Houses where they worshipped at Bainbridge, Hawes and Countersett, as well as the Schoolhouse and stable at Countersett, which they helped to establish. All the buildings survive bar the Meeting Houses at Hawes and Bainbridge (the present Meeting House is a later structure). These two buildings have had their history drawn entirely from documentary sources, as have two dwelling houses which have also disappeard, Verity House in Countersett and Coopermire Farm which stood in the field of that name above the road to Carr End.

Countersett Hall is a remarkable place with an atmosphere all its own, a feeling derived from a combination of peacefulness and activity at the centre of a busy Dales hamlet. The house, set in a fold of the hills below Countersett Crag, with its large low beamed rooms and small mullioned windows has welcomed people over the years as owners or tenants, servants, travellers or visitors. Each has left with a distinct impression of great age and a feeling for all that has gone before.

About 1250 the Anglo-French 'Cousbance' established his summer cow pasture or 'Vaccary' in a sheltered hollow in the Forest of Wensleydale which perpetuates his name as Countersett (Cousbance's Seter).[1] By 1280 it was known as Coustansate and was worth £13 6s. 8d.[2] Five years later its value had fallen to £7.[3] In 1301 the founder's son, Roger, paid £1 as Lay Subsidy (tax) being one fifteenth the value of his personal goods.[4] Countersett was worth £6 13s. 4d. in 1342 and is then lost from published records for 150 years. The vaccary was, in all probability, defined by the strong cam and ditch. This can still be traced

Countersett Hall's kitchen range with massive stone jambs, lintel and moulded mantelpiece, set between 18th century cupboards and panelling. The cast iron range (oven, side boiler, sooker stone and reckon) was taken out in 1957.

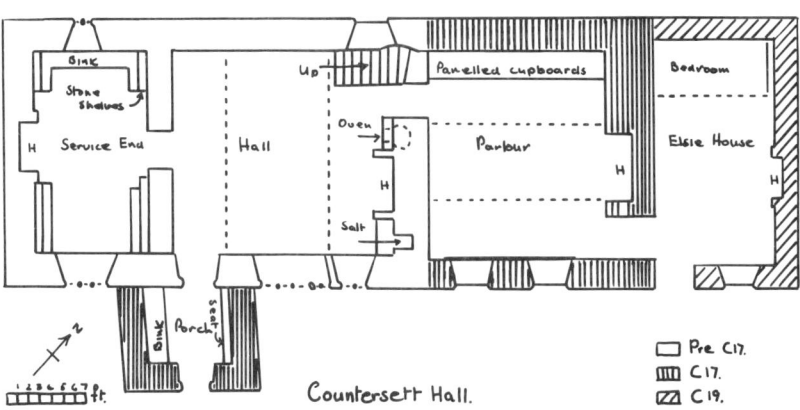

Plan of Countersett Hall showing the pre-17th century dwelling, with salt box and brick lined bread oven, to which Richard and Margaret Robinson came in 1650. Also their new parlour and porch. The later accommodation, called Elsie House, was occupied as a separate dwelling by Mrs. Scott, née Elsie Middlemas, c.1909.

from a point on the north bank of the River Bain near Gill Edge to Semerdale Hill Top. It continues along the watershed behind Semerdale House to the East Pasture top wall and along to a point above the Crag End limekilns from where it plunges down to Semerwater. Similar ancient embankments have also been noted round Marsett, Stalling Busk, Blean, Burtersett and Appersett.[5]

By 1605 the area within the boundary at Countersett had grown into a thriving village with 15 tenants, 13 houses, 297 acres of meadow and 192 pasture gates. The tenants paid a combined rent of £15 19s. 11¾d. a year. The principal ones were all called Metcalfe. There were two Harrisons, including a Bartholomew, but no Robinsons.[6] An undated survey of the Lordship of Middleham sets out the Raydaleside vaccaries as they were in about 1630 when they included Calfehouse alias Fallhouse, Countersett with Semerdale, Tongue, Marsitt, Stallen busk, [and] Radall.[7]

Richard and Margaret Robinson moved into one of the Countersett tenements in 1650. This dwelling survives within Countersett Hall. It comprised two rooms in the western part of the present house, that is to say the service end and the central hall. A fireplace stood at either end and a curved stair in a corner beside the main hearth. The house was lit by small mullioned windows. These survive in the original service end, near the hearth as a fire window and in the end wall of the washhouse where one has been reset. They were cut from soft coarse-grained sandstone which probably came from a local fell-top quarry. Each had two lights, bar that in the service end, which had three. The outline of the original roof was preserved in the central wall where it showed as a steeper pitch than the present one, and it may have been thatched.

Richard Robinson's rebuild gave us the house we see today. The eastern third is his entirely with its stone arched fireplaces, oak beams and fine ovolo mullions. His two three light mullioned windows in the parlour, it is said, were taken to Cupples Field at Bainbridge in 1885[8] when all the square paned leaded lights were removed.

The big stone porch, though not locked to the main house and having dissimilar corbels and labels, dates from Richard's time. The stone doorcase looks older than the 1650s and may well have been salvaged with the east bedroom fireplace, from the old house. A small stone inscribed R R·M 1650, which is set in the wall above the front door, recalls the first coming of Richard and Margaret Robinson to this place.

For 43 years, Richard occupied the house, and he died there in 1693. This period and that of Michael his son and heir who died in 1712, have already been covered. Michael's brother John followed but the date of his arrival is uncertain. Much of the woodwork and glass in the house suggest a considerable modernisation early in the 18th century but the details are not forthcoming. They may well be the work of John who, in time, 'being

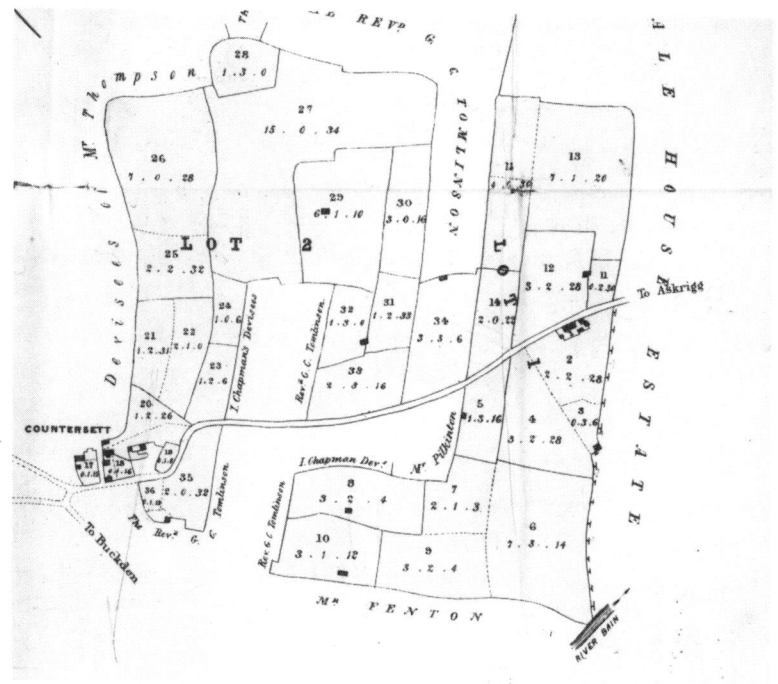

A plan of estates at Countersett Hall and Holly House by W. Monkhouse, York, endorsed on a deed of 2 December, 1853.

1 Holly House, outoffices and garden.
2 Goady Middles.
3 Goady Middles and barn.
4 Low Close.
5 Calf Close and barn.
6 Willow Mires.
7 Tongue Foot.
8 North Tongue and barn.
9 South Tongue.
10 South Tongue and barn.
11 Parrock.
12 Nook and barn.
13 Brackenslack.
14 Low Kettlewell.
15 High Kettlewell.
17 Board Inn, outbuildings and garths.
18 Countersett Hall, outoffices and garths or gardens.
19 Perr.
20 Calf Parrock or Firbank and barn.
21 West Woods.
22 Middle Woods.
23 Len Faw.
24 Wood.
25 Woods Head.
26 West Ing Head.
27 East Ing Head.
28 Coppy.
29 Thistlepott and barn.
30 Southerkeld.
31 Middle Borwins.
32 West Borwins and barn.
33 Low Borwins.
34 East Borwins and barn.
35 New Close and Frank Garth and barn.
36 Crag allotment adjoining 35.

now-grown old and well Stricken in years' died at Countersett in 1739. He left the house and farm to his eldest son Richard who lived on there with his brother John and other unmarried members of the family.[9] The bachelor brothers lived out their lives at Countersett Hall and were succeeded by Amos's widow, Jane Robinson from Semerdale, whom Samuel Nichols noted in the house in 1778.[10] She died at Carr End, the home of her daughter Hannah Fothergill, in 1794.

Harrisons had farmed Countersett Hall for several years and at Jane's departure or death Reuben Harrison moved in. At that time it was known as 'Courts' and was remembered as such by Daniel Harrison who was born in the house in 1795. He also preserved a memory of the garden set with flowers, terraced borders and snowdrops.[11] Reuben, as a conscientious Quaker, refused to pay tithe in 1794 and had one heifer distrained for the same.[12] The Harrisons left in 1802, Reuben, Senior, for High Blean where he died the following year,[13] and Reuben, Junior, with his children, for Crawshaw Booth, near Burnley. Marsden Monthly Meeting accepted them into membership, 17 June, 1802. Later the Harrisons moved on to Liverpool and became a prominent merchant family there.[14]

From 1802 Countersett Hall farm and house were occupied by John Tennant, who probably came from Langstrothdale, and published his intention of marriage with Elizabeth Thistlewaite 12 April, 1802.[15] The Tennants' time at Countersett passed virtually unrecorded but they are known to have been Quakers. Their tenancy ceased in 1851, the last year in which John paid a churchwarden's rate of 5s. 10d. for the farm,[16] a sign perhaps of the decline in strongly held Quaker principles. William Howitt came to Countersett in the 1830s and wrote that,

> We went, on the only Sunday which we passed in the dales, to his [George Fox's] favourite Meeting of Counterside, and could almost have imagined that the remarkable times of his ministry were yet remaining. We found the meeting amid a cluster of rustic cottages in pleasant Simmerdale, by Simmerdale Water. The house in which he usually lived during his visits to this valley adjoining the meeting; a true old-fashioned house, where the remains of his oaken bedstead were still preserved; and a very handsome one it must have been, and far too much adorned with the vanity of carving for so plain a man, and so homely a place.[17]

John Tennant was followed by George Paley who came from High Forse and moved in during 1852.[18] The Paley family is said to have been related to the Archdeacon Paley of Carlisle.[19] They established themselves at Countersett and stayed for all of 90 years. During this period they developed a widespread business as cheese and butter factors. John and Mary Paley were at Countersett 1872-83 and old George Paley died there in 1887.[20] The tenancy then passed to his sons

Joseph and Francis.[21] The brothers prospered in their business which centred on the Board Inn to which the local farmers brought their produce each Monday night and bartered cheese, butter and eggs for provisions. Joseph Paley contracted typhoid fever and died in 1890[22] whereupon Francis, hitherto of Holly House, moved in with his wife Hannah White whom he had married in 1882.[23] Hannah died but left a family from which the later Paleys are descended. Francis married twice more, firstly to Mary Cockburn from Aysgarth in 1892,[24] then to Ellen Sayer who retired with him to Bainbridge about 1920.

Thomas and Francis Paley followed their father at Countersett Hall and kept on the business as well as the farm. Many men and women in the Dale who worked on the farm in their day speak of a time when there were two or three hired men and a maid in the house with two Irish men sleeping in the meal chamber at haytime. The kitchen was thickly hung with sides of bacon and hams and the milk float was sent to Askrigg Station each day as liquid milk sales had replaced the cheese business to a certain extent. The farm men were roused at three o'clock in the morning to mow the Coopermire field in haytime. They used a double horse mowing machine and Paleys' old white horse was well known in the Dale. Both men and women worked in the hayfields and it was no rare thing to see a team of 10 people strewing a hayfield with hand rakes. Local boys were brought in to work the horses, as hay leaders. The stone flags outside the front door were swilled each Friday and the kitchen floor scrubbed. The ash hole beneath the hearth was emptied and whitewashed round. The weekly wash took a whole day using a set-pot in the wash-house across the flags. Baking, similarly, took a whole day and a white cat was known to curl up on the warm rising bread if not closely supervised. Visitors came and went all summer, many of them from Lancashire, recalling the mass exodus of Dalesfolk to those parts in the 19th century. The carol singers called at Christmas and were always welcomed with a drink and food at Countersett Hall.[25]

Tom Paley died in the house in 1942 and was succeeded by Mat and Lizzy Kilburn who, as Bell family relations, had lived at Holly House. They stayed until 1951 when Ernest and Margaret Hall moved in from Marsett. They removed the cast iron kitchen range in 1957 and installed a hot water system and a bathroom. In 1964 the stone flagged floors of the middle room and the porch were dug out and concreted. There was no systematic archaeological investigation but potsherds, cinders and rusty nails collected from the soil were dated and show continuous occupation from around 1250 to 1850.[26] The Halls bought Countersett Hall and the farm from Mrs. S. M. Ingeborg Flugel, William Pilkington's heir, in 1961 and lived there until December 1968. Jean and Arthur Dower, from Leeds, took possession from spring 1969 and began major repairs and alterations, including a new roof. The Dowers occupied the house whilst the farm was let off to Christopher (Kit) and Margaret Peacock. Their son, Brian Peacock, bought the land in 1987, Robin and Pat West having bought Countersett Hall from the Dowers in 1985.

Semerdale Hall

The word Semerdale is used in one medieval deed to describe the valley now known as Raydaleside.[1] By the early modern period 'Semerdale' was used only for the area between Countersett and Gill Edge and the farm now known as Semerdale Hall. By the 1630s the whole of Raydaleside was settled in hamlets and farms and a list of 'vaccaries', already quoted, includes those at Countersett, Semerdale and Tongue.[2] An area of fields below Holly House is still called Tongue but the name is used elsewhere in the Dale thus making a positive identification difficult on present evidence. There is no record of the first house at Semerdale but it was a substantial dwelling in 1690 when John and Elizabeth Robinson settled there. It was described as 'Semerdale House' when the births of their children were recorded in Quaker Registers between 1690 and 1710.[3] Henceforth, and throughout the 18th century, it was referred to in both formal and informal records as Semerdale or Semerdale near Countersett. John and Elizabeth Robinson lived at Semerdale to around 1715-20 when their son Amos took over both the house and the farm. He was living there in January 1727 when his father released the property to him. Amos Robinson gradually built up a fair sized holding which included not only Semerdale but the Thistlepots, Souterkeld and Borwins lands.[4] He brought his first wife, Ann Metcalfe, to Semerdale in 1729 but she died the following year. Amos married again, in 1747, when his bride was Jane the daughter of Joseph and Hannah Pratt from Holly House. They had four children, all born at Semerdale. It is not clear whether Amos lived out his life at Semerdale or at Countersett. His burial among Friends at Bainbridge records him as of Countersett but that may be taken to mean Semerdale. Thomas Jeffery shows 'Summerdale' on his map of 1772 along with Cooper Mire, Holly House and Counterside. Cooper Mire alone was spelt as now, but was misplaced on the map.[5]

John Robinson, the son of Amos, married in 1774 and settled at 'Semerdale Hall'. That term was first used in formal records when his daughter Margaret was born in 1775.[6] The Robinsons did not live at Semerdale much beyond 1778 but let both house and farm to Jonathan Shaw. The original lease survives and is a good illustratiion of 18th century landlord tenant relationships and good husbandry in respect of

> that Messuage House commonly called Semerdale House, with all Houses, Edifices, Buildings, Barns, Stables, Orchards, Yards, Gardens, Backsides, And all those Closes of Meadow and Pasture

Ground called Middle Semerdale, West-Mires, East Mires, Low Cornclose, Cornclose, East-Semerdale, West-Semerdale, Parrock, Nursery, Northtongue, Southtongue, Tonguefoot, and Lowclose, sixty-three acres in all with eight beast-gates in Bainbridgeside, five and a half on the Crag and five in Bardale Pasture.

All which said Premises now are or late were in the Tenure . . . of . . . John Robinson . . . to hold . . . unto the said Jonathan Shaw . . . for the full . . . term of seven years . . . paying therefore yearly . . . the clear Rent . . . of Forty five Pounds . . . Jonathan Shaw . . . shall and will . . . well and sufficiently keep in repair, uphold, Moss and point with Lime all the houses and buildings, and glazen all the windows therein, and also make, repair, plaish, cleanse and scour all the Walls, Fences and Ditches . . . and will . . . lay and spread all the Manure, Ashes . . . and will before the Expiration of the said Term of seven Years procure or burn spread and lay on Thirty Chalders of good Lime upon those closes or ground called West Semerdale and East Semerdale . . . in such manner as shall be most likely to improve the same.

The lease is dated 27 April, 1778.[7]

Samuel Nichols noted Jonathan Shaw at Semerdale in 1778[8] and the land tax list of 1781 records John Robinson's five tenants at Countersett thus:

Jonathan Shaw	£1. 3. 4.
Reuben Harrison	14. 0.
John Sill, Senior	14. 8.
John Sill, Junior	8. 0.
Thomas Metcalfe	2. 8.[9]

John Robinson gave Jonathan Shaw a receipt for 'his full Quota according to Covenant of Lime' in 1781 and that is the last we hear of him as tenant but he was still living at Semerdale when he married Eleanor Edgar at Busk in 1783. The next tenant was James Coates who took up residence in 1783. He was described as a widower of Semerdale when he married Ann Tomlin from Blean at Busk in 1786. James Coates' original lease has not survived but one for seven years from 1802 has. It shows him paying an annual rent of £70 with £10 per acre for land ploughed and £2 per load for hay sold off the farm. James and Ann Coates baptised children from Semerdale at Busk Church, 1786-1801, and moved to Holly House about 1809 or 1810.[10]

John and Mary Robinson returned from Bradford and they too lived at or in some part of Holly House. It appears likely that Semerdale was rebuilt for them at this time. The old house stood behind the replacement and its back wall survives as a retaining wall under the plantation with joist holes, stone shelves and a stone doorcase to a vaulted cellar. The new house was three storeys high with Venetian windows, stone architraves and a cornice. The big high rooms had wall alcoves and decorated plaster ceilings, six panelled doors and marble fireplaces. The wide elegant stone staircase had cast iron balusters under a wooden handrail.

There was set, in the gable end of the new stable range across the yard, a sculptured face in a stone frame. The face does not survive but sprightly black horses painted on the inside wall above the manger and beside the loft ladder, do and contribute to the considerable style of the buildings. The 'Surgery', and the washhouse with a billiard room over it, were built later, probably by the last John who resided at Semerdale from 1857. In c. 1898 the top storey was dismantled, due to bulging walls, and the roof timbers lowered onto reduced walls with the roof replaced. The bay windows formed no part of the original house and may date from 1857.

John and Mary Robinson moved into Semerdale House in 1812 or 1813 and stayed there until about 1816.[11] Mary Robinson is not heard of again and John returned to Bradford. There is no burial for Mrs. Robinson in Friends' records nor in the parish registers at Busk or Askrigg. She may of course have died in Bradford and was perhaps not a Friend. Certainly her marriage to John Robinson is not recorded in Friends' Registers. There is a tradition of a ghost of Semerdale Hall. The tale is told that Mrs. Robinson fell to her death at the foot of the stairs and that 'Dr. Robinson' walks the house still.[12]

Richard Thistlethwaite and his wife Agnes Hunter were the next tenants at Semerdale, from about 1816. Richard died in the house in 1820[13] and was succeeded by his son John from Shaw Cote. John Thistlethwaite was Clerk to Richmond Monthly Meeting in 1822 and it is clear that he had a very close relationship with the Robinsons and was appointed a trustee in the will of John Robinson.[14] A John White is noted as of Semerdale in 1831 but the Thistlethwaites were still the tenants and Agnes died there in 1834. John Thistlethwaite was married at Countersett Meeting House, aged 50 years, to Elizabeth Routh in 1839. He retired to Dale Grange in 1843, gave up the farm at Semerdale in 1844, and was succeeded by John Robinson and his second wife, the former Margaret Wood from Askrigg, in 1845.[15]

John and Margaret Robinson lived out their lives at Semerdale and died within two months of each other in 1853 leaving the property to their five sons, some of whom lived there for a time. They were each in turn bought out by the eldest, John,[16] who had John Baines as tenant in 1855-6,[17] but moved in himself in 1857.[18] The topographer Whellan saw the house at this time and described the Robinsons as one of the two oldest families in the Dale. The other was Thwaite at Low Foss.[19] In fact the age of the Robinsons was rapidly drawing to a close. In the summer of

Semerdale House as it was built about 1812 but with bay windows of a later date. The second storey was taken off about 1898. Print by W. Monkhouse, York, from the Sale Catalogue of 1862.

1862 John and his wife, Ann Elizabeth, removed to Thornesfield House, Thorne, near Wakefield. They sold Semerdale,[20] the last remaining part of the family estate to William Pilkington of Blackburn.

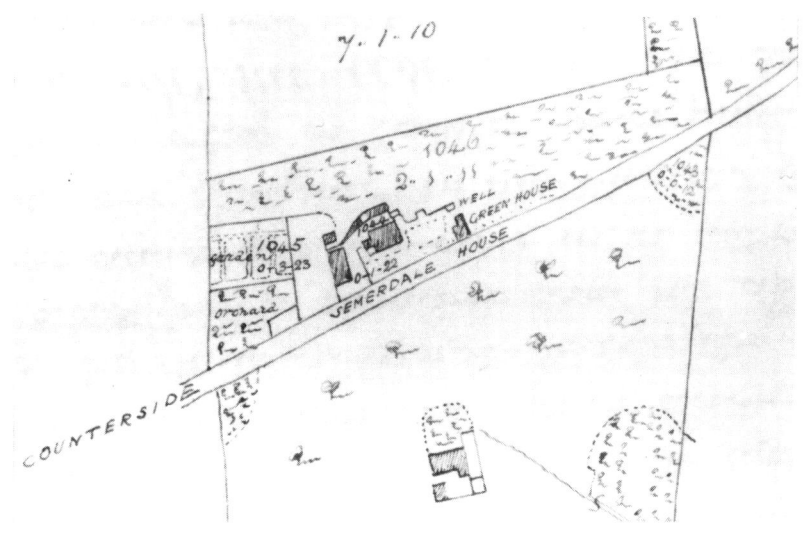

A plan of Semerdale House and grounds as drawn and endorsed on a deed of 29 December, 1862.

William Pilkington was Mayor of Blackburn, 1856-8, and his brother James Pilkington, M.P., owned the Swinithwaite Estate near Leyburn. William lived at Wilpshire near Blackburn,[21] and installed one James White at Semerdale House, 'that Capital Messuage or Mansion House', with its 92 acres of land, from 25 March, 1863. Within a year White had given it up.[22] The descent of the house is obscure for a time but it appears that the land was joined to Holly House. The Reverend Richard Wood, brother of Margaret Wood Robinson, lived at Semerdale in the 1870s. He was noted as M.A., 'Clerk without Cure', in 1871 and was still in the house in 1874. The most extraordinary tales are told of him and particularly that of his loosing a shotgun at a fir tree in the front garden. The tree was killed but not the good people of Raydaleside who made a wide detour up behind the house when he was at home.[23]

By 1883 Matthew Bell, of Holly House, had taken over all the land and moved into Semerdale House. He died there in 1890 and was succeeded by his wife Ann, who farmed to her death in 1899, and then by their sons William and Richard. Will died at Holly House in 1920 and

Dick farmed on to his death in 1936. The following year his nephew, Matthew Bell from Marsett, took over the tenancy and stayed on to buy Semerdale and Holly House from William Pilkington's heirs in 1958. Matt Bell died in 1976 and was followed by his son Matthew Bell with his wife Mary and their sons Matthew and Paul from Holly House.

Holly House, Boar Inn, Verity House and Coopermire

The farm called Holly House grew out of the Countersett vaccaries and may well represent the one called Tongue in c.1630. It came into Robinson hands but its course before 1712, when Michael willed it to Ephraim, is not recorded. At that time it comprised a dwelling house with 10 closes of land and 15½ cattle gates all in the occupation of Ephraim Robinson. It passed at Ephraim's death in 1735 to his brother John who had Richard Burton as tenant in 1739.[1] John left it by will to his youngest son Joshua Robinson who rebuilt the house, possibly as two livings, in 1740. His name and the date are carved on the keystone over the front door. Joshua was described as of Semerdale when he acted as Joseph Dobinson's executor in 1745.[2] Joseph and Hannah Pratt also lived at Holly House at this time and their daughter Jane married Amos Robinson in 1747. Hannah Pratt died at Holly House in 1752.[3]

Two years later, in 1754, Joshua Robinson, yeoman of 'Hollinghouse', was married to Elizabeth Hoyle at Marsden Meeting House[4] and returned to live and farm at Holly House. Thomas Lambert of Holly House was married to Ann Dent at Busk old church in 1755 but the Robinsons still lived there as well. Joshua had the fields called Tongues from his brother Richard in 1765 and in 1774 Richard Metcalfe of Holly House was married to Elizabeth Harrison of Semerdale at Aysgarth Church. One year later Joshua Robinson died at Holly House and left it to his nephew Joshua Blakey of Thorns House near Carr End.[5] He was in residence by 1778 and lived out his life as a gentleman. He died in 1800 and left the farm to his eldest son John who was something of a ne'er-do-well. In 1803, John Blakey, 'late of Edinburgh . . . now of . . . Manchester, Cotton Spinner', sold the 29 acre farm to his cousin John Robinson of Bowling, Bradford. Joshua Robinson Blakey, John Blakey's brother, was the tenant.[6] He appears to have lived in the house until 1809-10 when John and Mary Robinson occupied it for a few years before moving into the rebuilt Semerdale. Perhaps the west end of Holly House, with its plaster panelling (now decayed) was built for them around this time.

By 1814 the Coates brothers, John and Thomas, were in residence; they were staunch Methodists who played a major part in building the first chapel at Marsett.[7] Their father, James Coates, died at Holly House in 1820, and was buried in Busk churchyard where his gravestone, though badly decayed, can still be seen and read in a favourable light. His widow Ann kept the farm on in her own name and was noted as a farmer in 1823.[8] Their son Joseph and his wife Mary came next and baptised children from Holly House at Stalling Busk between 1824 and 1842.[9] Joseph's brother Thomas, born at Semerdale in 1796, and his wife Elizabeth emigrated to Canada about 1833-4 and took Thomas' mother Ann Coates with them. The old lady died in July 1849 and was buried at the Blue Church Cemetery near Maitland, Ontario, Canada, where a gravestone, not quite so badly decayed as that of James Coates at Busk marks the spot. Joseph Coates lived on at Holly House and was noted there in a deed of 1842, and on the Tithe Award and Map of 1843-4.[10]

By 1845 he had been replaced by Thompson Blenkiron from Marske in Swaledale who was married at Askrigg Church in 1842, and died at Holly House in 1860.[11] He was followed by George Preston, who acted as hind or farm bailiff to John Robinson,[12] and married Dorothy Paley from Countersett in 1860. In 1864 a Jane Gregson was married from Holly House, pointing perhaps to a second dwelling. Matthew Bell took over the tenancy of Holly House farm and the Semerdale land in 1862. He was married at Grinton Church in 1863 and brought his wife Ann to Holly House where their children were born 1865-72. In 1879 a Dorothy Smith from Holly House was buried at Busk, aged 64,[13] being perhaps, the 'old lady' whom the Bells say lived once in the west end. At some date before 1883 the Bells moved into Semerdale House and were replaced at Holly House by Francis Paley, who farmed with his brother Joseph, whom he succeeded at Countersett Hall in 1889 or 1890. Matt Bell's daughter Mary and son William, with their families, lived in the house in the 1890s and were succeeded by Matt Bell, Junior, from 1900-6. William Bell, elder brother of Matt, returned with his wife Annie and died in the house in 1920. Thereafter the tenants were Matt and Lizzie Kilburn, who took in visitors, 1920-37; Mrs. Rose Hannah Rossal, a great-great granddaughter of James Coates of Semerdale and herself a staunch Methodist, 1937-46; Malcolm and Flo Ross who came from Ashton under Lyne and made a beautiful garden, 1946-63; and Matthew M. Bell and his wife Mary who moved into Semerdale Hall in 1976 since which date Holly House has been let.

The house known as the Boar Inn, has been both a farm and an inn, the property of the Robinsons for decades, but we have no record of their original purchase. The first recorded inhabitants are Bartholomew Harrison and his wife Isabell Thompson who were married at Thomas Fawcett's house in Hawes in 1662.[14] That year they were both fined for Meeting illegally among Quakers in James Wetherald's house at Askrigg and the fact was recorded by their friend and neighbour Richard

Robinson.[15] In 1667 the house was rebuilt with their initials B H I and a Latin inscription on a square stone over the fire window. Bartholomew was a hosier, that is a man who bought and sold wool and knitted hose. He had a field or two including the Tong Paddock in Blean and several cattle gates where he kept a little stock, including four horses, indispensible to a travelling man such as he.

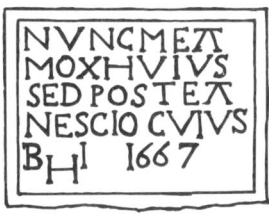

Boar Inn date stone showing the Latin inscription 'NUNC MEA MOX HUIUS SED POSTEA NESCIO CUIUS' which translates as, 'now mine, once thine, but whose afterwards I do not know.' Also the initials of Bartholomew and Isabell Harrison and the date 1667.

There is nothing to suggest that the house was an inn in the 17th century but Bartholomew was known to take a drop too much to drink at times. He regretted his weakness, especially when Richard Robinson threatened to take the Meeting from his house. When Bartholomew died in 1685 he left £5 to the poor and needy Quakers of Bainbridge, Askrigg and Thornton Rust and the house to Isabell for as long as she needed it. Henceforth history is silent until 1738 when John Robinson was in possession and left the property as New Close House, to his son Richard. Richard's will of 1765 has it occupied by Reuben Harrison who was probably, but not certainly, a descendant of Bartholomew and Isabell. In 1752 Reuben Harrison and Hannah Smith, both of Countersett, were married in the church at Stalling Busk. Reuben is mentioned in Amos Robinson's will of 1775,[16] and moved into Countersett Hall about 1790, from where his son, another Reuben married Margaret Thompson in 1794.[17]

For the next 30 years the thread is lost but by 1820 the house was certainly an inn and it appears as such in the Quarter Sessions records under 'Raydaleside. James Thwaite, Innkeeper, Board', an entry which was repeated until at least 1829. In 1823 the Raydaleside public house was given as William Airey's 'Masons Arms' and in 1840 it was Thomas Metcalfe's 'New Inn'.[18] This last was almost certainly at Stalling Busk. By 1843 John Tennant held the Board Inn as an appurtenance to Countersett

Hall, where he lived, as tenant to John Robinson, who owned both. In 1853 it was described as a 'House used as an Inn, Outbuildings and Garths'.[19] The landlord about this time was Peter Beresford from Raisgill who married Hannah Paley from Countersett Hall at Busk in 1854. The Beresfords left in 1874.[20] Bulmer noted the Board Inn of Thomas Brunskill in 1890 as did Kelly in 1893.

The 'Bardale Meeting', which met each spring to regulate the commons of Marsett village, used the Board Inn at Countersett every year from 1879 to 1898. In 1899 and 1900, they met at the Boar Inn, Countersett, the same venue, but a slight change in the sign. They paid five shillings for the use of the room.

Alice Brunskill was landlady of the Boar Inn from 1903 to 1907 after which it passed to her son Simon Brunskill. He kept it as the Boar Inn to 1920 when the licence was given up.[21] Henceforth it was occupied as a farmhouse first by John (Jack) Hodgson and his wife Jinny to 1927, then by Fred Kirkbride and his wife Elsie, who was a Quaker and took in visitors, until they left for Bainbridge in 1954. George and Vera Thornborrow came next followed by William and Ellen Metcalfe to 1959. Percy and Ann Webster from Wood End bought it in 1960 and lived there until 1969 when it was sold to Arthur and Jean Dower of Countersett Hall who have let it to various tenants.

Verity House also stood in Countersett and was owned by the Robinsons. It may have taken its name from the Verity family, two of whom, Richard and Roger, witnessed the will of Bartholomew Harrison in 1685. It probably stood between the Meeting House and Low House Farm on the site now occupied by a ruined barn, or it may even have been an alternative name for Countersett Hall. The description would fit such a conclusion but this is not borne out in the records. It was probably the cause of the dispute between John Robinson and James Metcalfe in 1717 and is mentioned in detail in the wills of John Robinson, 1739, and that of his son John in 1775.[22]

Coopermire Farm disappeared from the maps more than 120 years ago but it was a well known farm in its day and probably took its name from Edmund Coultherd who lived at Countersett and baptised children at Askrigg Church between 1705 and 1721. John Metcalfe lived there in 1747 and baptised a child at Busk Church that year. Alexander Fothergill recorded Coopermire as the home of John Fawcett in 1754 when he paid him for work he undertook on the Richmond to Lancaster Turnpike Road in Greenscarmire. John Fawcett of 'Cowper Mire' was married at Busk in 1757, baptised his children there and was buried in the old churchyard in 1764.[23] Richard Robinson mentioned the farm in his will of 1765[24] and it is marked on Jeffrey's map of 1772 but in the wrong place.[25] Greenwood's map shows it in the correct place as Cowper Mire in 1816. Christopher Mires lived there in 1778 and in 1813 Walter Middlemas, who had lived at Busk many years before, died at Coopermire, was buried at Busk and is the last known resident. By the time that the Robinsons parted with the Countersett estate in 1853, Coopermire had been absorbed into Countersett Hall farm as a field called 'High Cow Foot Mire with the site of a house & barn thereon.'[26] Today all that remains is a length of the back wall with blocked windows and a doorway in the wall between the Coopermire Field and the Cowpasture above the road to Carr End.

PART IV

One Meeting House for all

Bainbridge Friends Meeting House

HAD THE ORIGINAL FRIENDS MEETING HOUSE at Bainbridge survived it would have been one of the oldest in the country, having been bought as a cottage, 7 December, 1668 and subsequently used for Meetings. Elizabeth Routh and Dorothy Todd gave Ann Coward £13[1] for it. It stood on the site of the present Temperance Hall and that building contains some of its materials. In 1672 the Quakers added a plot of land on Holme Bray, at the opposite end of the village, to be used as a Burial Ground.[2]

There is no record of the arrangements in the cottage Meeting House but as the years went by the minute books show Friends making alterations and arrangements for their comfort. In 1684 they paid 2s. 6d. rent for a stable for their horses whilst they were at Meeting and Michael Pratt was given 1s. to be 'disbursed concerning the Stable w[hi]ch Fr[ien]ds use at Bainbridge.' In 1685 John Stockdale and John Aira were asked to have the Meeting House repaired but the job dragged on until 8 June, 1686 when 'Will Mason & Joseph Scott are desired to bargain with some to bring ling for thatching the Meeting House at Bainbridge.' In September they paid 13s. 4d. for '6 Cartfull of Ling & 5 Cartfull of seave thack & Leading & Theaking of the same . . . [and in November] . . . paid to Will: Mason for thatching the Meeting House 6/4 by Mich: Robinson on . . . behalf of the Meeting.' Hearth tax cost the Quakers 1s. 5d. in 1687 and minor repairs cost them 6s. the following year.

In July, 1687 Friends in Wensleydale generally were considering building a Meeting House at Hawes but those 'without Hawes quarter . . . are unwilling that one Meeting House for all be built in Hawes Quarter'. Edmund Harrison and Michael Robinson were appointed to make alterations at Bainbridge in 1688 and in November 1689 a collection was made to pay for repairs and to purchase a 'Beare' for the use of the Meeting. In 1689 the Meeting House was licensed by Quarter Sessions as a place for Quaker worship. More repairs in 1691 cost 14s. and on 12 December, 1694, Friends met 'and concluded to Purchase a place for a Meeting House.'[3]

Thus, on 25 November, 1696, Quakers bought the old house next to the existing Meeting House from Thomas and Stephen Nicholson for £6 10s.[4] They also had by gift, the entry or passageway at the east end of Nicholsons' house. The passageway and Nicholsons' house were incorporated into the new Meeting House[5] which came into use 5 October, 1697, for the 'people residing in or about Bainbridge & Raydaleside.'[6] Hawes Friends went on alone to make their own arrangements in 1698.

A note of 6 July, 1709 shows 'Something being proposed in Relation to Repairing the old Meeting House at Bainbridge for Containing the Womens Meeting and Stabling, fr[ien]ds Agrees that it be done Accordingly.' John Robinson and John Fothergill were to supervise the work. In 1713 they paid a fee farm rent for the Meeting House and the following year Joseph Dobinson was 'desired to buy firr deals etc: and get the Gallery in Bainbridge Meeting House seated therewith.' Ephraim Robinson and others were appointed to make repairs in 1720 and again in 1732. There is a note that 'The Charge of Bainbridge Meeting House in the year 1733 Respecting the making a New Gallery for Inlarging the said House and some other Repairs amount to £10. 18. 8'. On 5 September, 1739 'Joseph Dobinson is Desired to Get the Meeting House Mossed & limed where Necessity seems to Require it.' The work cost 6s. 3d. Thatched roofs were not mossed, so far as is known, therefore, it is reasonable to assume that the Meeting House by then had a stone flagged roof. Further improvements were made in 1756 when money was given for the Meeting House to 'be floored with Boards and half the seats well Backt'. Richard Robinson and others were instructed to make further repairs and to alter some seats in 1760.[7] On 16 January, 1774 Alexander Fothergill of Carr End wrote in his diary that it was 'First day and Meeting at Bainbridge, but a Snow being Now fallen So that the Ise is hide, I durst not venture to Bainbridge.'[8] The Meeting Houses at Countersett and Bainbridge were 'wanting repairs' in 1822.[9]

Henceforth, little is known of Bainbridge Meeting House until the 1830s when rising prosperity and aspirations caused the local Friends to see their old building as inadequate. 'The Friends Appointed to attend to the repairs of Bainbridge Meeting House have suggested the propriety of Building a New One in a better situation to which this Meeting acceeds.' They chose a new site beside the Burial Ground at Holme Bray and built a new Meeting House there in 1836. The previous one was sold for £42 in 1842.[10] The purchaser is not known but the building was used by the Congregationalists until they too built a new chapel in 1865. The Band of Hope and Temperance Society[11] used it, then virtually rebuilt it in a totally different form in 1910. A contemporary note from the *Darlington and Stockton Times* tells of the money raising events and reopening, 16 December, 1910.[12] Local memories speak of a chapel-like interior with

Bainbridge Friends Meeting House with original windows and stove pipe, c.1890.

a tiered floor and altar rails which were taken out to make room for badminton when the building became the Village Hall. The architect was Fred Rowntree of York.

The new Friends Meeting House of 1836 was a totally different creation. It was built with new materials on a virgin site just to the north of the old Burial Ground. It stood in the field called High Holme-bray, near to the 'Calffy-yate' [Calf-gate] which had been left to Friends by the prominent Bainbridge Quaker, Joseph Dobinson, in 1745. Dobinson, described variously as schoolmaster, yeoman and shopkeeper had bought up his small estate at Holme Bray in small pieces, as houses, gardens, garths, closes and cattle gates between 1714 and 1738. He died and left all his property, with half his shop goods, to Richard and John Robinson of Countersett in Trust for Friends, 'for repairing their Meeting Houses, stables and burying grounds, or any other service'.[13]

No accounts survive for the new building work but the Meeting House shows itself to be the product of a well thought-out scheme professionally executed. The resulting accommodation included a large, light and airy Meeting room with a raised Elders' bench and ministers' gallery against the east wall. This room could seat around 100 people. An ingenious construction of folding doors and sliding shutters could, on special occasions, open up accommodation for 100 more seats in the passageway, the womens' Meeting room beyond and in the loft above it. This last, reached by a flight of wide stone steps, with a beautifully turned baluster, is tiered to give its occupants a good view of the Meeting in progress below. Wensleydale Preparative Meeting moved into this building in 1836. Some 17 members were present at Meeting on Census Day in 1851.[14]

Bainbridge Meeting for Worship has met continuously from the winter of 1652-53 to this day and Friends still meet each Sunday within 50 yards of the spot where Richard Robinson, their Meeting's founder was buried almost 300 years ago.

Hawes Friends Meeting House

Hawes had an important and active group of Quakers from an early date led and chiefly motivated by Oswald Routh and Thomas Fawcett. Meetings and marriages are recorded at Thomas Fawcett's house from 1662 and at Oswald Routh's from 1671. Oswald Routh maintained a private Burial Ground for Quakers, in a corner of his Corn Close, from at least 1670[1] and gave it to them by will in 1681.[2] Throughout the 1690s there was considerable discussion about the provision of Meeting Houses in Wensleydale, as the Meetings had outgrown the use of private houses and the old converted cottage at Bainbridge. On 7 October, 1690, Preparative Meeting considered building at Hawes but the plan was delayed and the following year they paid 5s. for repairs to the house they used in the town.[3] It was not until 1698 that Oswald Routh sold them a dwelling house adjoining his Brunt Acre House for conversion to a Meeting House. It cost £10[4] and the Declaration of Uses of 1711 shows that it was demolished at once and a new Meeting House erected on the site.[5] In 1702 they instructed 'Richard Taylor . . . [to buy] . . . 6 Load of Coals . . . for the use of the particular Meeting' and in 1709 James Wetherald was asked to supply oats for Friends' horses at Hawes.[6] They were building a stable of their own in 1737 and there is a note that Amos Robinson settled 'The Charge of Repairing Haws Meetg House and Altering of the Gallery in the year 1735 [which] amounted to £5. 5. 8½.'[7] The old messuage house at the west end of the Meeting House was bought from the Rouths for £2 10s. in 1746 and rebuilt, the upper part as an addition to the Meeting House, the lower part as a stable.[8] A porch was added at the front of the Meeting House.

Hawes Friends seem to have had an obsession with stabling, perhaps as a direct result of the rising importance of Hawes as the market centre for Wensleydale. On 3 July, 1772 they 'Paid to Oswold Routh one years Rent for the additional part of the Meeting House Stable at Hawes 0 : 5 : 0.' The provision was proving inadequate again and is mentioned

2 July, 1786, thus another piece of land was bought from Oswald Routh, at the north west corner of the Meeting House, and further stabling built there. A note of 1 October, 1786, mentions 'The Alterations to the Meeting House stable at Hawes' and another its completion by 3 December. By 13 February, 1787, the Quakers considered the property complete and drafted a new trust deed. This set out the whole as the Quaker Meeting House at Hawes with the stable and a chamber over it, probably used as the womens' Meeting, with a porch and a small parcel of ground to the front. There was also a newly built stable on the north west corner of the Meeting House and a parcel of enclosed ground called the Quakers Burial Ground nearby.[9]

By 1815 the condition of the Meeting House was giving Friends cause for concern and five of them were appointed to survey the fabric, 14 May, 1815. They delivered their report 12 November following. It showed the roof and the floor of the building to be in very bad condition and the Meeting House too small to accommodate 'such of the neighbours as incline to attend.' They recommended that the front wall be taken down

Hawes Friends Meeting House with Meetings for Worship every Sunday at 10.30 am and 6.30 pm, 'All Seats Free', and an Adult School for men every Sunday at 4.30 pm. Photograph by Norman Penney [?] c.1886.

and rebuilt further out, the floor and the roof both to be raised and relaid, and shutters to be inserted in the womens' Meeting room wall so that they might be opened when extra room was required.[10] The report was duly accepted, the work ordered, completed, and in part paid for by the sale of the Whitcliff allotment near Richmond in 1817.[11] Henceforth little is known until 17 October, 1838 when Hawes Meeting was officially discontinued and the last family of Quakers, the Hunters of Swineley, transferred to the Meeting at Lea Yet in Dent.[12]

In 1866 Mary Metcalfe, schoolmistress, of Hawes rented a room in the Meeting House as a private school[13] and in 1874 Thomas Weatherald of Askrigg supplied three new doors.[14] The Meeting made little or no headway up to 1882 when Norman Penney arrived in the Dale as a Friends Missioner, a position he occupied for four years during which he injected new life into the Society and made Hawes the centre of his work. All the Meeting Houses round about were reopened with enthusiasm, lectures given, courses arranged, Meetings encouraged wherever possible, and an Adult School formed at Hawes. A measure of his personal success can be seen in the mass of applications for membership which came into Richmond Monthly Meeting at this time.[15] Much of Norman Penney's later published work shows his intimate knowledge of the area and the gravestone of his first wife and son remain in Friends' ground at Hawes.

The Triennial Report for 1895 shows that the expansion of the previous decade had not continued. A Particular Meeting still functioned in the town with a Friends' Mission Room and a childrens' First Day School at Appersett. The Adult School had ceased. The Preparative Meeting at Hawes shared the same problems as those at Bainbridge and Carperby which together reported that:

> the number of members is now 40, as compared with 48 three years ago; the decrease of 8 is accounted for by 6 deaths & 8 removals out of the Mo. Meeting, while the admissions have only been 6 viz. one by birth, two by convincement, and three by Certificate of Removal: of the present members 5 are practically non resident, and these are all young showing that the exodus of young people from the Dale still continues. Except at Carperby those in Membership do not constitute half the Congregation that Meets for Worship in our Meetings, and at Hawes the proportion is much less. The number of Attenders reported three years ago was 55, the present number is 55 which includes 4 belonging to the allowed Meeting at Appersett.[16]

The latter had been started in 1891 and reported to Yearly Meeting the following year. Very little is known of its activity but it functioned throughout the 1910s and there are accounts for paying rent, rates and a caretaker at Appersett up to 1922. The burial ground nearby, being Sandemanian, was not used by Quakers. In 1896 Friends built a small toilet block in the front garden of the Meeting House at Hawes. It cost £300 and represented a considerable investment for that date.[17]

In 1906 the Quakers still met at Hawes each Sunday at 10.30 am and 6.30 pm[18] and continued to meet, though less frequently, to about 1930. The Meeting House at Hawes was closed officially and the fact conveyed to Yearly Meeting in 1932.[19] The North Riding County Council bought the property for £600 in 1933 after which it stood empty or was let until the summer of 1955 when it was demolished to make way for a new road.[20]

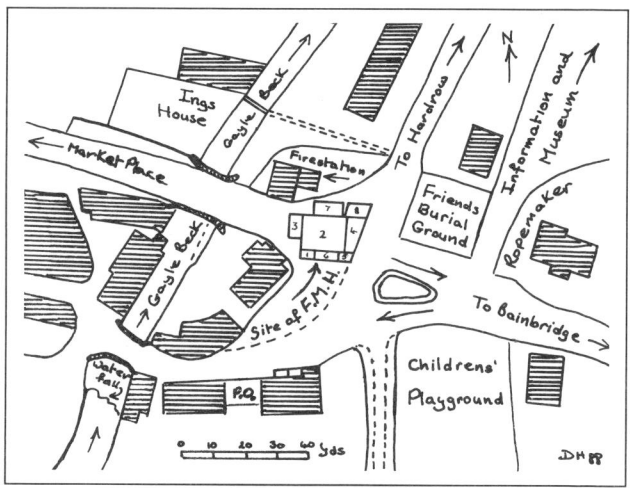

A sketch plan of the Friends Meeting House and Burial Ground at Hawes. The Burial Ground remains but the Meeting House was demolished in 1955. It stood about 20 yards south-east of the present fire station where the road now lies. 1 = porch, 2 = Meeting House, 3 = stableloft, 4 = dwelling, 5 = toilets, 6 = yard, 7 and 8 = stables.

Countersett Friends Meeting House

Both the older Meeting Houses in Upper Wensleydale are now demolished. Countersett remains and is the one most closely associated with the Robinsons, as it was built originally by Michael in or about 1710. His father, Richard Robinson, established the first Wensleydale Preparative Meeting in his own house at Countersett and made that the real centre of Quaker activity in the Dale for all of 50 years. Meetings were held in the house, marriage ceremonies were performed there, and many early Friends stayed with the Robinsons including George Fox and Richard Hubberthorne.

Countersett Friends Meeting House interior as completed in 1778 with the preacher's pulpit used by Primitive Methodists a century later.

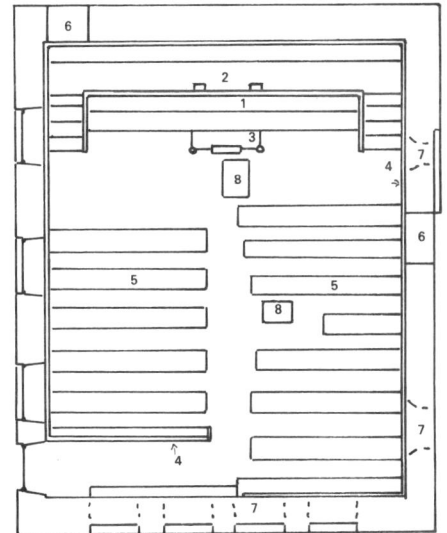

Countersett Friends Meeting House plan showing the layout in 1778 with the Elders' bench (1), ministers' gallery (2), and the pulpit installed by Methodists later (3). Note pine panelling throughout (4), two ranks of loose benches (5), blocked doorways (6), blocked windows from the earlier buildings (7) and flagstones set in or on the wooden floor where stoves stood (8).

Shortly before his death, Michael Robinson transferred Countersett Meeting from his home to the Meeting House he had specially built from pre-existing buildings on the site. His new building of c.1710 survives but was much altered in 1778-9. Its original layout cannot now be discovered. The four blocked windows in the north east wall date from 1710, but the front wall is of the later alterations. The ministers' gallery and Elders' bench may have stood in their present position, or have backed onto the front wall as at Brigflatts.

There survives in the Quaker archive an account of 1732 which shows that an upper floor was put in at that date. The account details the cost of beams, joists, floorboards and nails in sufficient quantity to cover the entire room. Richard Terry did the work and it cost £14 4s. 4d.[1] The new upper room was entered by a door on the south west end at first floor level which, owing to the steep fall of the ground across the site, made it ground level at that point. The earlier windows, at intermediate height, were blocked by the new floor level and new ones were made in the back wall. That wall also had a broad ledge, to take the joist ends, and may previously have supported a loft. Again we have no record of the internal arrangements. The front windows were altered later but original doorways survive at both the back and the front and the ground floor may well have been used as a stable for visiting Friends' horses.

This was the local Meeting House for the Fothergills of Carr End and two of their sons came this way, Samuel in August 1758 and Doctor John in August, 1763; both came to Meeting but neither has left a description of what he saw.[2] John Woolman, the famous American Friend, came to Countersett in September, 1772 and wrote in his diary, 'Sixth of ninth month the first of the week. – I was this day at Counterside, a large Meeting-house, and very full. Through the opening of pure love, it was a strengthening time to me, and I believe to many more.'[3]

In 1760 Richard Robinson, Alexander Fothergill, Thomas Blakey and Jeffrey Lonsdale were altering seats and making repairs at Countersett and Bainbridge,[4] but the building at Countersett continued to deteriorate until 1777 when a 'very Considerable & Expensive Repair' had to be made.[5] The Robinsons were either unable or unwilling to pay for this work therefore Friends, having maintained the place for many years, paid for the work and had the freehold conveyed to them for 10s. in 1778.[6]

It looks from the surviving structure as if a collapsing front wall was the chief problem and that it was completely demolished and rebuilt with three tall twelve paned sash windows at intermediate height. All the other windows and doorways bar one were blocked up and the wooden floor of 1732 brought down to ground level. The upper half of the back wall was covered with a lath and plaster stoothing and a ceiling of the same material was put in. Previously there had been no ceiling for wooden pulleys, for hanging lamps, remained in the roof until 1977. A stove stood on a flag let into the wood floor with a stove pipe or chimney flue let into the south west end wall. The whole was finished with a new ministers' and Elders' bench, wall panelling and a low speer or screen, all nicely moulded in pinewood. Benches of the same wood stood loose in two parallel rows. Thus was made the Meeting House we see today.

In 1781 Thomas Lambert and Joshua Blakey were appointed to make the necessary repairs to the Meeting House doors and to take in the 'land Given for a courting or yard',[7] which they duly completed. A large flag was placed in front of the door and a cobbled yard, with tidy gateposts and a sturdy wall, could also be entered by way of a pillared stile from Countersett Hall Garth. Flags replaced the cobbles in the 1960s.

The increasing drift of people from the Dale, and the strict rules against Quakers marrying out, took their toll and Countersett Meeting began to die. In 1812 one of its members, Robert Blakey, was disowned and deprived of his membership for 'joining himself in Marriage contrary to our Rules.'[8] That year Friends had agreed to divide the Wensleydale Preparative Meeting between Hawes and Countersett[9] and in 1814 Countersett disappears from the minute books as a regular meeting place.[10] Since then Quakers have used it only occasionally but they were contemplating repairs in 1822 and it was officially discontinued after Richmond Monthly Meeting reported, 15 July, 1846, that

> The representatives from Wensleydale inform this Meeting that the altered situation of a number of its members renders it desirable that that Meeting which has for a considerable time been held at Counterside, should in future be held at Bainbridge, to which alteration this Meeting agrees.[11]

William Howitt came to a Meeting at Countersett in 1836 and wrote, with an amount of truth which it is impossible to check, that

> the people were flocking from all sides, down the fells, along the Dales, to the Meeting, not only the Friends themselves, but other Dalespeople; and we found Mr. John Pease, brother of the M.P., and his lady, from Darlington, addressing a crowded audience. The old times of Fox seemed indeed returned. The preachers discourse was one of an earnest and affectionate eloquence, and the audience was of a most simple and unworldly character. Almost every person, man or woman, had a nosegay in hand; nosegays in truth, for they very liberally and repeatedly applied them to the organ whence they are named. The herbs, for they consisted rather of herbs than flowers, were as singular as the appearance of such a host of nosegays itself. Not one of them was without a piece of southernwood, in some instances almost amounting to a bush, and evidently there entitled to its ancient name, 'lads'-love and lasses'-delight.' With this was

grasped in many a hardy hand, thyme, and alcost, and in many, mint! No doubt the pungent qualities of these herbs are found very useful stimulents in close and crowded places of worship, and especially under a drowsy preacher, by those whose occupations for the other six days lie chiefly out-of-doors, in the keen air of hills and moors. That such is the object of them was sufficiently indicated by a poor woman who offered us a little bunch of these herbs as we entered the Meeting-house, saying with a smile, 'they are so reviving'.[12]

The Meeting House was also known to Jessie Fothergill of the Carr End family, who published a novel, *Kith and Kin*, set in the area, and into which she incorporated some family traditions. In it she wrote,
'At last she came to the dip in the road, which, with its shade of overhanging trees, its quaint nestling old houses and cottages, and tiny whitewashed Friends' Meeting House, was known as Countersett . . . Up and down the little paved courtyard they paced, feeling vaguely that this quiet and peace in which they now stood was not to last for ever; that the tiny square Friends' Meeting House, where the silence was disturbed, it might be once a week, perhaps not so often, by a discourse, or a text, or an impromptu prayer from some Friend whom the spirit moved to utterance of his thoughts.'[13]

Jessie Fothergill, though she published her book in 1881, wrote of a period nearer the beginning of the century when the Meeting House was approaching the end of its active life. In time the Primitive Methodists came to use it for their meetings but the Quakers looked after it. They repaired slates and windows in 1858-60 and in 1868 paid James Metcalfe of Marsett £4 4s. 6d. for more repairs. They also published notices of meetings called at Countersett and other places, for Alfred Wyatt in 1874 and paid for more repairs in 1875.[14] The Primitive Methodists were certainly using the Meeting House by 1872 and in 1883 Norman Penny of the Hawes Mission held meetings and noted in his diary that 'The Primitive Methodists hold services at Counterside first day evening.'[15] In fact the Primitives installed a pulpit which they fixed to the front of the Elders' bench, moved the stove into the middle of the room, and drafted an official Trust Deed for their use of the building in 1893.[16]

In 1895 the Friends reported that 'At the request of Friends from a distance, who have been visiting us, several Meetings have been held in the Meeting House Countersett – the Primitive Methodists are allowed the use of this Meeting House for a nominal sum, but it is available for the use of Friends whenever desired.'[17] In 1903 Methodist services were held at 2 pm and 6.30 pm each Sunday[18] but later this was altered to one afternoon meeting with a Sunday School. The chapel was reckoned to have 120 sittings in 1909-17 and about 40 attenders, a figure which had fallen to about 30 by 1921.[19]

Numbers continued to fall to and after the Methodist Union of 1932 when the distinction of 'Primitive Methodist' disappeared. A new roof was provided in the 1920s. The building was redecorated and electric light installed in 1955, when the highly ornamented brass hanging oil-lamps were removed. The 1960s brought electric overhead heating in place of a big iron stove. A massive overhaul in 1977-8 included a new roof and windows, redecoration throughout and the removal of the Methodist pulpit and most of the old benches. The pulpit and one bench are now in the Upper Dales Folk Museum at Hawes. The Methodists withdrew in 1977 but Friends' Meetings for Worship are usually held on the first Sundays of summer months.

Countersett School

There is no record of a formal school on Raydaleside until Friends built one at Countersett in the 1770s. Previously the curate at Stalling Busk had on occasions offered tuition in the chapelry but such work was rare and spasmodic.[1] Friends had been considering the provision of a school as early as 1759 when Doctor John Fothergill wrote to his brother Alexander at Carr End to ask, 'How does your School at Countersett go on? I am ready to assist whenever I am called upon, if it cannot be otherwise supported.'[2] Perhaps the venture had already begun on a small scale in the Meeting House, as often happened within an active and generous Meeting. The full story may never be known but Richard and John Robinson were somehow prompted to leave money to support a schoolmaster at Countersett in 1765 and 1777 respectively.[3]

The decision to build a stable with a schoolroom above it was taken in 1768 but the actual building work was delayed until at least 1772. When complete the school appears to have been run on non-denominational lines but of its organisation, teachers, finance or scholars before 1782 we know nothing. In that year Friends met at Hawes and heard that 'Rob: Glover Being Gon to teach School at Counterset again which Step Seems to Be to Friends Satisfaction at present.'[4] Friends also considered their dissatisfaction with John Robinson for not delivering his uncles' bequests to the school, a matter they pursued for many years before finally abandoning it, unresolved, in 1795.[5]

History is silent again for a long period. Jessie Fothergill mentions it in her novel *Kith and Kin* as remembered by her relation at the beginning of the 19th century. She wrote of Judith who had

> heard her great-uncle tell how he and his sister, her mother's mother, used to go to school at a queer little brown house in the said hamlet, trudging with hornbook and slate in hand from Scarr Foot [Carr End] to Counterside, and back again. She noticed spikes of wild

The Friend's school at Countersett as constructed about 1772. It had a stable in the basement from the beginning and a flagged courtyard from 1861.

arum, black briony, yellow hawkweed, lilac scabious, blue veronica, honeysuckle, hips and haws, and berries as broad flat tufts left by the wild guelder rose

in the hedge by the roadside.[6]

In 1816 Robert Blakey of Countersett, a great, great, great grandson of Richard Robinson, was schoolmaster in the village and there can be little doubt that this was his school. He married Anne Coates of Holly House in 1811, joined the Church of England, was curate of Ecclesfield in West Yorkshire, and in 1821 emigrated to Canada as a medical missionary.[7]

The school appears again in the minutes of Richmond Monthly Meeting, 16 February, 1825. 'It has been suggested that considerable pecunary advantage may acrue this Meeting by appropriating a small sum of money from its funds, not exceeding £10 to the encouragement of a suitable Schoolmaster at Counterside. And after considering the subject this Meeting appoints the following friends to make necessary enquirey and engage a suitable person for one year Viz – Alex: Fothergill, Thos: Blakey, John Thistlethwaite.' On 16 June following, 'Alex: Fothergill reports, that friends appointed to make enquiry for a suitable Schoolmaster at Counterside have attended thereto, and engaged a young man for one year with the salary of Eight Guineas.'[8]

The next master of whom there is a record was William Thistlethwaite who was born at Swineley Farm, Widdale, in 1813, the son of Richard and Margaret (Hunter) Thistlethwaite. William was educated at Lea Yet in Dent and at Ackworth. He then became an apprentice clogger and leather cutter with his uncle James Thistlethwaite at Bainbridge. When he was 18 he was drawn towards teaching and began his career at Countersett school, which he taught from 1831 to 1834, before moving on to schools at Penketh, Ackworth and Wilmslow.[9] William White's Directory for the North Riding in 1840 noted the Society of Friends 'Chapel and School' at Countersett and Richard Routh as schoolmaster on Raydaleside.[10] Thus another man drawn from the local Quaker community began a teaching career at Countersett school. Richard Routh was born at Field Gate near Bainbridge in 1815, the son of William and Mary (Grainger) Routh. William had been disowned by Quakers for marrying out but this did not prevent his son from teaching in the Quaker school. Richard, like Robert Blakey, was a farmer. He lived near Bainbridge and is said to have walked up to the school each day. He left in 1842 to become the first principal of Sibford Quaker College in Oxfordshire.[11]

The first edition of the Ordnance Survey map, at six inches to one mile, surveyed in 1854 and published in 1856, shows both Meeting House and school at Countersett. The 1851 census includes Christopher Metcalfe, farmer and schoolmaster, then aged 27, at Countersett. He also acted as census enumerator.[12] His family remain in Wensleydale and recall that he was not a Quaker but that this was his school and that he lived at the house called Boar Inn.[13] By 1861 he had given up the teaching post to either Mrs. Jane Brunskill 'School Mistress' of Marsett or Richard Carter 'Schoolmaster' of Blean.[14] Another local man John (Jack) Outhwaite whose wife was a Metcalfe, is said to have taught there about this time and immediately prior to James Mudd.[15]

Between 1858 and 1861 Friends carried out minor repairs to both the school and the Meeting House. In 1861 William Webster received £2 5s. 6d. for flagging the yard before the school and from the beginning of 1862 James Mudd had a 'subscription' of £3 per annum.[16] He was not a Quaker but the son of an Anglican farmer at Marsett. He took the schoolhouse from Friends in his own right for an annual rent of 2s. from year to year, in an agreement dated 6 April, 1869.[17] He was noted as 'School Master', aged 33 years and the only teacher on Raydaleside in the census of 1871.[18] Kelly mentions him and the 'day school' at Countersett in 1873.[19] The Quakers continued to pay him a subscription up to 11 July, 1874 and it is remembered that his total income was £60 for the year.[20] In 1873 the Bainbridge school building committee had sought Friends permission to enlarge the school 'in accordance with the requirements of the Government.' The trustees were unable to grant a building lease but agreed to let the premises at a nominal rent provided 'the school be continued as heretofore on an undenominational basis.'[21] The scheme fell through and the new school, when it was built, was at Stalling Busk and under the auspices of the Church of England. James Mudd transferred himself, his school and scholars there in the autumn of 1874.

The next and last recorded teacher at Countersett was Fanny Shaw who applied to Richmond Monthly Meeting, in August 1875, to open a school for girls and small boys at Countersett Meeting House and to have the schoolhouse adapted as a cottage.[22] The plan was agreed and Friends duly paid Fanny Shaw the £3 annual subscription for teaching and Thomas Weatherald £8 15s. 5d. 'for Partitioning a Bed Room off Countersett School House and one Newe outer door & jambs for the same.'[23] There is no record of Fanny Shaw after 1875, when the 'subscription' ceased. The recollections of an old lady in Bainbridge in the 1940s relate of her walking as a child, from Bainbridge to Countersett school each day and learning to knit.[24] The stable continued to be used by Friends who paid John Paley of Countersett Hall 8s. for corn for their horses kept there during Meetings. They were also in receipt of 10s. being one half year's rent from John Scott for Countersett schoolhouse.[25] Henceforth the cottage was let off until Friends sold it in 1963.

Abbreviations for Notes and References

Digest.	Digest of Births, Marriages and Burials, Yorkshire Quarterly Meeting of the Religious Society of Friends (Quakers), Friends House Library, London.
FHLL.	The Library of the Religious Society of Friends, Friends House, Euston Road, London, NW1 2BJ.
FPT.	*The First Publishers of Truth,* edited by Norman Penney (Supplements 1-5 of the *Journal of the Friends' Historical Society*), 1907.
Fox, 1836.	*A Journal or Historical Account of George Fox,* sixth edition. Printed by Anthony Pickard, Leeds, 1836.
Fox, 1925.	*The Short Journal and Itinerary Journals of George Fox,* edited by Norman Penney, C.U.P., 1925.
Fox, 1952.	*The Journal of George Fox,* revised edition by John Nickalls, C.U.P., 1952. L.Y.M.
LCLA.	Leeds City Library, Archives Department, Sheepscar Branch Library, Chapeltown Road, Leeds, LS7 3AP.
MMM.	Monthly Meeting Minutes.
NYCRO.	North Yorkshire County Record Office, County Hall, Northallerton, DL7 8AD.
PMM.	Preparative Meeting Minutes.
PRO.	Public Record Office, Chancery Lane, London, WC2A 1LR.
Semerdale Deeds.	Manuscript deeds of Semerdale House and farm on loan from M. Bell of Semerdale Hall.

Notes and References

Introduction *(pages xii-xvii)*
1. Winthrop S. Hudson, 'A Suppressed Chapter in Quaker History', *The Journal of Religion*, XXIV, 1944, p. 114.
2. *Fox*, 1952, p. VII.
3. *Fox*, 1952, p. 104.
4. *FPT*, p. 311.
5. *Fox*, 1836, pp. 489-501.
6. *Fox*, 1925, p. 226.
7. *FPT*, loc. cit.
8. Op. cit., p. 312. Brotherton Library, Leeds, Yorkshire Quarterly Meeting, VI. 18, Testimonies, 1687? – 1901.
9. *Yorkshire Archaeological Society Journal*, IX, 1886, p. 193. Aldborough Parish Register.
10. NYCRO, R/Q/R 1/164, Richmond PMM. Prior to 1752 the calendar commenced on Lady Day, 25 March (old style dating). Early Quakers preferred the use of numbers to 'heathen' names, so March was the First month of the year. In this account all dates except those used as quotations, have been revised to New Style.
11. John Fothergill, *An Account of the Life and Travels in the Work of the Ministry*, 1676-1744, 1753, p. 10 (London, Luke Hinde).
12. Brotherton Library, Leeds, Yorkshire Q.M. I.11, Testimonies, 1710-1845.

The First Quaker in Wensleydale

The Man Convinced *(pages 1-6)*
1. *The Parish Register of Wensley in the County of York*, 1538-1700, The Yorkshire Parish Register Society, 108, 1939, passim.
2. NYCRO, Z 97/1, Redmire Deeds.
3. *Wensley*, op. cit., p. 20.
4. *FPT*, p. 311; 'an Heiris' may be read as either 'an heiress' or 'Ann Heiris'.
5. *Wensley*, op. cit., p. 34.
6. *FPT*, loc. cit.
7. Op. cit., p. 307 & 312. Brotherton Library, Leeds, Yorkshire Quarterly Meeting, VI. 18, Testimonies, 1687? – 1901.
8. Op. cit.
9. Ernest E. Taylor: *The Valiant Sixty*, passim. (Sessions Book Trust, York, 1988).
10. *FPT*, p. 312.
11. Ernest E. Taylor, *Richard Hubberthorne Soldier and Preacher*, 1911, p. 15.

12 *FPT*, pp. 307-10; Taylor, 1911, loc. cit.
13 *FPT*, p. 312.
14 William C. Braithwaite, *The Beginnings of Quakerism*, p. 150. (Wm. Sessions Ltd., York, 1981). FPT, p. 313.
15 Op. cit., pp. 148-51. FHLL, Adverse Box W, *A Further discovery*, etc., Gateshead, 1654. Brotherton Library, Leeds, Yorkshire Q.M., VI, 18.
16 FHLL, Digest of Births.
17 NYCRO, R/Q/R 8/1, Rental, n.d.
18 NYCRO, ZPG 6/3/1, Rental, 1661.
19 Semerdale Deeds, Schedule of Title Deeds and Writings relating to Semerdale House Estate, c.1862.
20 NYCRO, ZPG 6/1/1, Conveyance, 9 November, 1663.
21 NYCRO, ZPG 4/1, Account.
22 NYCRO, ZPG 4/2, Accounts.
23 PRO, E 179/216/462, Hearth Tax, 1673, Bainbridge.
24 Derived from title deeds, probate records, maps and fieldwork.
25 LCLA, Richard Robinson's probate inventory, 1694. Archaic or dialect words used for livestock include: Twinter = two winters old. Stirk = one year old calf. Tup = ram. Five Shear = five times shorn. Wether = castrated ram. Hog = lamb from first weaning to first shearing.

Continuing Faith *(pages 6-11)*

1 William C. Braithwaite: *The Beginnings of Quakerism*, 1923, p. 512.
2 *Fox*, 1952, p. 534. Footnote re. Henry Jackson of Mealhill near Hepworth, West Yorkshire. He built Totties Hall, Wooldale, c.1682.
3 *FPT*, p. 313.
4 NYCRO, R/Q/R 13/1, Memoranda Book of Sufferings.
5 Richard Robinson: *A Blast blown out of the North*, 1680, pp. 11-13.
6 J. C. Atkinson (ed.): *North Riding Quarter Sessions Records*, VI, pp. 61-7.
7 F. W. Parrott: 'Three Hundredth Anniversary of the Kaber Rigg Plot', *Cumberland and Westmorland Herald*, 26 October, 1963.
8 Norman Penney: *Extracts from State Papers relating to Friends*, 1913, pp. 176-77.
9 *Calendar of State Papers, Domestic Series, of the Reign of Charles II, 1663-1664*, 1862, pp. 337-38, 369. Marie Hartley and Joan Ingilby: *Yorkshire Village*, 1953, p. 84.
10 William C. Braithwaite: *The Second Period of Quakerism*, 1961, p. 12 & 615.
11 LCLA, RD/C 2, Archdeaconry of Richmond Correction Book, 1664.
12 Joseph Besse: *A Collection of the Sufferings of the People called Quakers*, 1753, pp. 122-23.
13 Richard Robinson, op. cit., p. 43.
14 Joseph Besse, loc. cit.
15 NYCRO, R/Q/R 2/4/1, Conveyance, 7 December, 1668.
16 NYCRO, R/Q/R 2/4/2, Conveyance, 17 May, 1672.
17 FHLL, Digest of Burials.
18 NYCRO, R/Q/R 2/4/29 & 49, 2/16/9 – 10, Mortgage, 14 September, 1709, Assignment, 18 March, 1738, Conveyance, 5/6 December, 1780.
19 William C. Braithwaite, 1961, op. cit., p. 302.
20 LCLA, RD/C11, Archdeaconry of Richmond Correction Book, 1679.

[21] William C. Braithwaite, 1961, op. cit., p. 309; FHLL, MS Vol. 101/38, Letter from Margaret Fell to her daughters, 31 March, 1677.
[22] *Fox,* 1925, p. 226.
[23] *Fox,* 1836, p. 234; FHLL, William C. Braithwaite, 'Calendar of the Swarthmore Manuscripts', Crossfield, 329/95/A; *Friends' Quarterly Examiner,* 36, 1902, p. 263; *Journal of the Friends' Historical Society,* 2, 1905, p. 23.
[24] *Fox,* 1925, pp. 226-27.

Sufferings and Other Exercises. *(pages 11-19)*
[1] Richard Robinson: *A Blast blown out of the North,* 1680, pp. 44-5; NYCRO, R/Q/R 13/1, Memoranda Book of Sufferings.
[2] *FPT,* p. 313. Humphrey Wharton of Gilling Wood Hall and Thomas Craddock, the Recorder of Richmond Borough, 1676-1688, were elected Members of Parliament for Richmond, 13 February, 1679. The case is not mentioned in either Lords' or Commons' Journals.
[3] NYCRO, R/Q/R 5/13, Letter c.January, 1681.
[4] NYCRO, R/Q/R 1/185, Wensleydale PMM.
[5] NYCRO, R/Q/R 4/25, Register of Sufferings.
[6] NYCRO, R/Q/R 1/185, Wensleydale PMM; Archaic or dialect words, Ling is Heather (Calluna vulgaris). Seave is Soft Rush (Juncus effusus). Thack = thatching material. Hearth Money = Hearth tax.
[7] The Philip Swale Manuscripts were withdrawn from the Richmond Monthly Meeting archive in 1907 and kept with Friends' records in London until 1966 when they were reunited with the original collection, from Carperby Meeting House, at the County Record Office, Northallerton.
[8] LCLA, Francis Smithson's will, 1670. Arthur Raistrick: *The Wharton Mines in Swaledale,* NYCRO Publications No. 31, 1982, passim.
[9] NYCRO, R/Q/R, Philip Swale correspondence, passim.
[10] NYCRO, R/Q/R 2/1/1, Philip Swale's will; W. Pearson Thistlethwaite: *Yorkshire Quarterly Meeting, 1665-1966,* 1979.
[11] Semerdale Deeds, Rachel Robinson's receipt, 16 March, 1687.
[12] J. C. Atkinson (ed.): *North Riding Quarter Sessions Records,* VII, pp. 102 & 198; op. cit. VIII, p. 164 & 243.
[13] NYCRO, R/Q/R 4/9, Testimonies against payment of tithe.
[14] FHLL, Digest of Burials. Brotherton Library, Leeds, Yorkshire Quarterly Meeting, VI. 18, Testimonies, 1687?-1901.
[15] George Fox: *Gospel Truth Demonstrated,* 1706, pp. vi-vii.
[16] NYCRO, R/Q/R 14/1, Marriage Certificate, 1692.
[17] *FPT,* pp. 308 & 314.
[18] Brotherton Library, Leeds, Yorkshire Quarterly Meeting, VI. 18. *FPT,* p. 314.

Later Generations

Faith and Prosperity *(pages 20-28)*
[1] Christopher Whaley: *History of Askrigg,* 1890, p. 82; NYCRO, ZPG 7/1/1, Lease 27 April, 1706.
[2] NYCRO, R/Q/R 1/185, Wensleydale PMM.

[3] Loc. cit.
[4] J. C. Atkinson (ed.): *North Riding Quarter Sessions Records*, VII, p. 70.
[5] NYCRO, QSB, 19 January, 1697, Presentment.
[6] NYCRO, R/Q/R 2/4/13-14, Conveyance, 18/19 January, 1778.
[7] LCLA, Michael Robinson's will and inventory, 1712.
[8] NYCRO, R/Q/R 1/185, Wensleydale PMM.
[9] LCLA, Michael Robinson's will, 1712.
[10] NYCRO, R/Q/R 16/32, Accommodation list, n.d.
[11] NYCRO, 1/185, Wensleydale PMM.
[12] NYCRO, QSB, 14 February, 1722, Presentment.
[13] LCLA, Ephraim Robinson's probate inventory, 1735.
[14] FHLL, Digest of Births.
[15] Semerdale Deeds, Mortgage, 8 January, 1711; Release, 24 December, 1731.
[16] NYCRO, R/Q/R 1/185, Wensleydale PMM; 6/19, 16/25 & 30, letters re. dispute and arbitration.
[17] NYCRO, R/Q/R 1/186, Wensleydale PMM.
[18] LCLA, John Robinson's will, 1739.

The Last of the Yeomen *(pages 29-36)*

[1] Semerdale Deeds, Mortgage, 8 January, 1711.
[2] Ibid, Deed Poll, 11 January, 1727.
[3] Ibid, Release, 24 December, 1731, Deed Poll, 3 December, 1738, Deed Poll, 17 May, 1739.
[4] LCLA, John Robinson's will, 1739.
[5] North Riding Registry of Deeds, G. 667. 515, Conveyance, 25 March, 1740.
[6] Ibid, AC. 249. 331, Conveyance, 6 September, 1756.
[7] LCLA, John Robinson, loc. cit.
[8] NYCRO, R/Q/R 1/186, Wensleydale PMM.
[9] Marie Hartley and Joan Ingilby, David S. Hall and Leslie P. Wenham: *Alexander Fothergill and the Richmond to Lancaster Turnpike Road*. NYCRO Publications, No. 37, 1985, pp. 48 & 50.
[10] Thomas Crosfield (ed.): *Memoirs of the Life and Gospel Labours of Samuel Fothergill*, 1843, p. 78.
[11] FHLL, Morning Meeting Minute Book, 5, pp. 102-03; John Fothergill: *An Account of the Life and Travels in the Work of the Ministry*, 1753, p. 306.
[12] NYCRO, R/Q/R 2/20/7, Declaration of Uses, 15 October, 1756.
[13] NYCRO, R/Q/R 4/34, Register of Sufferings.
[14] NYCRO, QDE(L), Land Tax, 1759.
[15] LCLA, Richard Robinson's will, 1765.
[16] NYCRO, R/Q/R 10/214, Bridge account, n.d., c. 1765-75.
[17] NYCRO, R/Q/R 1/186, Wensleydale PMM.
[18] NYCRO, R/Q/R 1/187, Wensleydale PMM.
[19] NYCRO, R/Q/R 2/4/12, Assignment of Term, 31 December, 1772.
[20] Christopher Whaley: *History of Askrigg*, 1890, p. 83.
[21] Semerdale Deeds, Conveyance, 30 May, 1770.
[22] Borthwick Institute, York, Amos Robinson's will, 1775.
[23] LCLA, Joshua Robinson's will, 1775.
[24] FHLL, Digest of Marriages.
[25] LCLA, John Robinson's will, 1777.

[26] NYCRO, ZPO 1/7, Sam(ue)l Nicholes List of the Inhabitants in the Chapelry of Busk in July 1778.
[27] FHLL, Digest of Marriages and Burials.

Conviction Fades and is Lost *(pages 36-41)*

[1] C. C. Booth: 'William Hillary – A Pupil of Boerhaave', *Medical History*, VII, October, 1963, pp. 297-316; B. C. Corner and C. C. Booth, *Chain of Friendship. Selected Letters of Dr. John Fothergill*, O.U.P. 1971.
[2] H. R. Hodgson: *The Society of Friends in Bradford*, 1926, p. 57.
[3] William Cudworth: *Histories of Bolton and Bowling*, 1891, pp. 296-98.
[4] H. R. Hodgson, op. cit. p. 114.
[5] Bernard Thistlethwaite: *The Thistlethwaite Family*, 1910, p. 81.
[6] NYCRO, R/Q/R 2/4/13-14, Conveyance, 18/19 January, 1778.
[7] NYCRO, R/Q/R 1/120, Richmond MMM.
[8] Semerdale Deeds, Lease, 27 April, 1778.
[9] FHLL, Digest of Births.
[10] Bradford Central Library, Miscellaneous MSS, Series B, 500.
[11] The Bradford Directory, 1792.
[12] Holdens' Triennial Directory, 1809, 1810, 1811.
[13] H. R. Hodgson, op. cit., pp. 132-33.
[14] William Cudworth, op. cit., p. 299.
[15] NYCRO, ZPM 1/2, Grant of Reversion, 1 September, 1803.
[16] Semerdale Deeds, John Robinson's will with probate annexed, 27 February, 1811.
[17] *The Leeds Mercury,* Saturday, May 25, 1811.
[18] Semerdale Deeds, Settlement, 28/29 February, 1820; NYCRO, PR/ASR, Askrigg Marriage Register.
[19] West Riding Registry of Deeds, IX. 608. 600; FHLL, Digest of Births; William Cudworth, op. cit., pp. 296-99; Semerdale Deeds, Birth Note for Richard Robinson, 1824, Baptism Certificate for Jeffery Wood Robinson, 1831, Conveyance, 28/29 February, 1820; Bradford Central Library, Miscellaneous MSS, Series A, 500; NYCRO, ZPM 1/11-12, Mortgage, 20/21 April, 1830, 1/13, Affidavit, 22 May, 1830, 1/18, Mortgage, 6 February, 1837, 1/27, Further Charge, 26 June, 1852.
[20] Semerdale Deeds, Deed Poll, 18 April, 1853; NYCRO, ZPM 1/22, Mortgage, 19 July, 1841, 1/23, Assignment, 26 April, 1842, 1/25, Assignment, 30 July, 1845, 1/29, Conveyance, 26 November, 1853.
[21] *The Medical Directory,* 1861, p. 572.
[22] Semerdale Deeds, Conveyance, 18 May, 1857, Conveyance, 31 December, 1857, Conveyance, 3 April, 1858, Trust Deed, 29 December, 1862.
[23] Semerdale Deeds, Mortgage, 26 March, 1862.
[24] PRO, RG9/3671, Census 1861.
[25] G. Whellan, *History and Topography of York and the North Riding*, 1858, p. 404.
[26] Semerdale Deeds, Conveyance, 29 December, 1862. *Yorkshire Gazette,* 5 July, 1862.

²⁷ Abigail D. Curkeet: *The Circuit Rider*, Mount Herob, USA, 1980, p. 71. PRO, RG9/3671, Census 1861. NYCRO, R/Q/R 3/23, Burial Note Book. Marie Hartley and Joan Ingilby: *Yorkshire Village*, 1953, p. 145. Semerdale Deeds, Mortgage, 19 April, 1853, Conveyances, 18 May & 31 December, 1857, 3 April, 1858. Personal communication, Margaret Rigoll and Margaret Elliott.

Stones and Mortar

Countersett Hall *(pages 42-48)*

¹ Percy Utley: 'An Old-World Dale', *The Dalesman*, 13, August 1951, pp. 222-25.
² 'Yorkshire Inquisitions', I, *Yorkshire Achaeological Society, Record Series*, 12, 1892, p. 225.
³ Loc. cit., II, op. cit., 23, 1898, p. 37.
⁴ 'Yorkshire Lay Subsidy of 1301', op. cit., 21, 1897, p. 89; J. Caley and S. Ayscough: *Taxatio Ecclesiastica Angliae*, Records Commission, 1802.
⁵ D. S. Hall, unpublished fieldwork.
⁶ T. S. Willan and E. W. Crossley: 'Three Seventeenth Century Yorkshire Surveys', *Yorkshire Archaeological Society Record Series*, 104, 1941, pp. 111-12.
⁷ London Guildhall Record Office, Royal Contract Estates, Middleham Survey, c.1628, Rental Box 4.5.
⁸ Amy Greener: *A Lover of Books* – The Life and Literary Papers of Lucy Harrison, 1916, pp. 25-6.
⁹ LCLA, John Robinson's will, 1739.
¹⁰ NYCRO, ZPO 1/7, Sam(ue)l Nicholes List of the Inhabitants in the Chapelry of Busk in July 1778.
¹¹ Amice Macdonell Lee: *In Their Several Generations*, Interstate Printing Corporation, Plainfield, New Jersey, USA, 1956, pp. 87-95.
¹² NYCRO, R/Q/R 4/36, Register of Sufferings.
¹³ FHLL, Digest of Burials.
¹⁴ NYCRO, R/Q/R 12/12, Certificate of removal; Amice Macdonell Lee: op. cit., passim.
¹⁵ NYCRO, R/Q/R 6/51, Letter.
¹⁶ NYCRO, PR/STB 2, Stalling Busk Churchwardens' Accounts.
¹⁷ William Howitt: *The Rural Life in England*, 1838, pp. 299-300.
¹⁸ NYCRO, PR/STB 2, Churchwardens' Accounts.
¹⁹ Oral tradition.
²⁰ NYCRO, PR/STB, Burial register.
²¹ Thomas Bulmer: *History, Topography, and Directory of North Yorkshire*, 1890, p. 349.
²² Paley family gravestone at Stalling Busk.
²³ NYCRO, PR/GR, Grinton Marriage register.
²⁴ NYCRO, PR/AY, Aysgarth Marriage register.
²⁵ Oral tradition.
²⁶ Pottery identified by Mrs. H. E. Jean Le Patourel, through the good offices of Mr. Sidney Jackson, late Keeper of Bradford Museums, 1965-66.

Semerdale Hall (pages 48-53)

1. 'Yorkshire Feet of Fines, 1218-1231', *Yorkshire Archaeological Society Record Series,* 62, 1922, pp. 2-4.
2. London Guildhall Record Office, Royal Contract Estates, Middleham Survey, c.1628, Rental Box 4.5.
3. FHLL, Digest of Births.
4. Semerdale Deeds, Deed Poll, 11 January, 1727, Deed Poll, 17 May, 1739, Conveyance, 30 May, 1770.
5. Thomas Jefferys: *Map of Yorkshire,* 1772.
6. FHLL, Digest of Births. Both 'House' and 'Hall' were used subsequently.
7. Semerdale Deeds, Lease, 27 April, 1778.
8. NYCRO, ZPO 1/7, Sam(ue)l Nicholes List of the Inhabitants in the Chapelry of Busk in July 1778.
9. NYCRO, QDE(L), Land Tax, 1781.
10. NYCRO, PR/STB, Stalling Busk, Marriage and Baptism registers; Semerdale Deeds, Lease, 5 May, 1802.
11. FHLL, Digest of Births; NYCRO, ZIF 73, Conveyance, 12 November, 1815.
12. Oral tradition.
13. Bernard Thistlethwaite: *The Thistlethwaite Family,* 1910, p. 80.
14. NYCRO, R/Q/R 6/66, Letter, 17 July, 1822, ZPM 1/29, Conveyance, 26 November, 1853, 1/30-31, Statutory Declaration, 2 December, 1853.
15. Bernard Thistlethwaite, op. cit., pp. 80-83; NYCRO, ZPM 1/29, 30-31, ibid.
16. Semerdale Deeds, Conveyances, 18 May, 1857, 31 December, 1857 and 3 April, 1858.
17. NYCRO, PR/STB 2, Churchwardens' Accounts.
18. Semerdale Deeds, Conveyance, 31 December, 1857.
19. G. Whellan: *History and Topography of York and the North Riding,* 1858, p. 404.
20. Semerdale Deeds, Conveyance, 29 December, 1862.
21. W. Abram: *History of Blackburn,* 1877, p. 402; F. Boase: *Modern English Biography,* VI, 1921 (1965 ed.), p. 399.
22. NYCRO, ZPM 1/37, Surrender of Lease, 1 July, 1863.
23. PRO, RG 10/4870, Census 1871; Edward Kelly: *The Post Office Directory of the North and East Ridings of Yorkshire,* 1872, p. 92, NYCRO, PR/STB 2, loc. cit.

Holly House, Boar Inn, Verity House and Coopermire (pages 53-57)

1. LCLA, Michael Robinson's will, 1712, John Robinson's will, 1739.
2. NYCRO, R/Q/R 2/20/1-2, Joseph Dobinson's will and probate, 1745.
3. FHLL, Digests of Marriages and of Burials.
4. FHLL, Digest of Marriages.
5. NYCRO, PR/STB, PR/AY, Stalling Busk and Aysgarth Marriage registers; LCLA, Richard Robinson's will, 1765, Joshua Robinson's will, 1775.
6. NYCRO, ZPO 1/7, Sam(ue)l Nicholes List of the Inhabitants in the Chapelry of Busk in July 1778. ZPM 1/1, Copy will of Joshua Blakey, 22 May, 1800, 1/2, Conveyance, 1 September, 1803.
7. Harry Holroyd (ed.): *Methodism in Wensleydale 1765-1965,* Leyburn, 1965, p. 23.

8 Edward Baines: *History, Directory and Gazetteer of the County of York, II, East and North Ridings*, Leeds, 1823, p. 508.
9 NYCRO, PR/STB, Baptism register.
10 Anna Jean Heard: *Journey into the Past*, Islington, Ontario, Canada, 1968, passim. Anna Jean Heard: *The Blakeys of Wensleydale*, 1969, passim. NYCRO, ZPM 1/23-24, Assignments, 26 April & 31 May, 1842; Bainbridge Tithe Apportionment and Map, 1843-44. Fred and Joyce Roberts: *The Township of Bainbridge in the Middle of the Nineteenth Century*, NYCRO, Publications No. 21, 1979, pp. 39-107.
11 NYCRO, ZPM 1/25, Assignment, 30 July, 1845, 1/29 Conveyance, 26 November, 1853. PR/ASR, Askrigg Marriage and Burial registers.
12 PRO, RG 9/3671, Census 1861.
13 NYCRO, PR/STB, Baptism, Marriage and Burial registers. PR/GR, Grinton Marriage register. PR/STB 2, Churchwardens' Accounts.
14 FHLL, Digest of Marriages.
15 Richard Robinson: *A Blast blown out of the North*, 1680, p. 12.
16 LCLA, Bartholomew Harrison's will, 1685, John Robinson's will, 1739, Richard Robinson's will, 1765. NYCRO, R/Q/R 13/1, Memoranda Book of Sufferings. PR/STB, Marriage register.
17 Borthwick Institute, York, Amos Robinson's will, 1775.
18 NYCRO, QDL(V), Registers of recognizances, 1822-29. Edward Baines, loc. cit. William White: *History, Gazetteer and Directory of the East and North Ridings of Yorkshire*, Leeds, 1840, p. 610.
19 NYCRO, Bainbridge Tithe Apportionment and Map, 1843-44. ZPM 1/29, loc. cit.
20 Oral tradition; NYCRO, PR/STB, Marriage register.
21 Thomas Bulmer: *History, Topography, and Directory of North Yorkshire*, 1890, p. 349. Edward Kelly: *The Post Office Directory of the North and East Ridings of Yorkshire*, 1893, p. 30. Bardale Meeting Minute Book, 1877-1900, with the Secretary of the Meeting. NYCRO, PS/HW 6/1, Register of Licences, 1903-20.
22 LCLA, Bartholomew Harrison's will, 1685, John Robinson's will, 1739, John Robinson's will, 1777.
23 NYCRO, PR/ASR, Baptism register. PR/STB, Baptism, Marriage and Burial registers. Marie Hartley and Joan Ingilby, David S. Hall and Leslie P. Wenham: *Alexander Fothergill and the Richmond to Lancaster Turnpike Road*, NYCRO Publications, No. 37, 1985, pp. 30 & 40.
24 LCLA, Richard Robinson's will, 1765.
25 Thomas Jefferys: *Map of Yorkshire*, 1772. Christopher Greenwood: *Map of the County of York*, 1817.
26 NYCRO, ZPO, 1/7, loc. cit., PR/STB, Burial register. ZPM 1/29, Conveyance, 26 November, 1853.

One Meeting House for all

Bainbridge Friends Meeting House *(pages 58-61)*

1 NYCRO, R/Q/R 2/4/1, Deed Poll, 7 December, 1668.
2 NYCRO, R/Q/R 2/4/2, Feoffment, 17 May, 1672.

[3] NYCRO, R/Q/R 1/185, Wensleydale PMM.
[4] NYCRO, R/Q/R 2/4/5, Feoffment, 25 November, 1696.
[5] NYCRO, R/Q/R 2/4/7, Declaration of Uses, 9 May, 1700.
[6] NYCRO, R/Q/R 1/185, Wensleydale PMM. 2/4/7, Declaration of Uses, 9 May, 1700.
[7] NYCRO, R/Q/R 1/185-186, Wensleydale PMM. 2/20/7, Trust Deed, 15 October, 1756.
[8] Marie Hartley and Joan Ingilby, David S. Hall and Leslie P. Wenham: *Alexander Fothergill and the Richmond to Lancaster Turnpike Road*, NYCRO Publications, No. 37, 1985, p. 101.
[9] NYCRO, R/Q/R 1/121, Richmond MMM.
[10] NYCRO, R/Q/R 1/122, Richmond MMM.
[11] Christopher Whaley: *History of Askrigg*, 1890, p. 67.
[12] *Darlington and Stockton Times*, 24 December, 1910, p. 3.
[13] NYCRO, R/Q/R 2/20/1-2, & 7, Joseph Dobinson's will and probate, 16 September & 21 December, 1745, Trust Deed, 15 October, 1756.
[14] Religious Census, 1851.

Hawes Friends Meeting House   (pages 61-64)
[1] FHLL, Digest of Marriages and Burials.
[2] NYCRO, R/Q/R 2/9/1, Declaration of Uses, 11 September, 1745.
[3] NYCRO, R/Q/R 1/185, Wensleydale.
[4] NYCRO, R/Q/R 2/9/4, Conveyance, 24 March, 1698.
[5] NYCRO, R/Q/R 2/9/5, Declaration of Uses, 7 March, 1711.
[6] NYCRO, R/Q/R 1/185, Wensleydale PMM.
[7] NYCRO, R/Q/R 1/186, Wensleydale PMM.
[8] NYCRO, R/Q/R 2/9/2-3, Conveyance, 12 & 13 February, 1787.
[9] NYCRO, R/Q/R 1/188, Wensleydale PMM; Conveyance, 12 & 13 February, 1787.
[10] NYCRO, R/Q/R 1/189, Wensleydale PMM. 16/44, Report on the fabric, 12 November, 1815.
[11] NYCRO, R/Q/R 1/121, Richmond MMM.
[12] NYCRO, R/Q/R 1/122, Richmond MMM.
[13] NYCRO, R/Q/R 2/9/8, Agreement, 1 September, 1866.
[14] Dobinson Trust Account Book, 1858-1932, consulted at Carperby Meeting House, c.1974.
[15] FHLL, MS. Vol. 176, 'Narrative of the Friends Mission in Hawes and Wensleydale' by Norman Penney, 1882-86. NYCRO, R/Q/R 1/124, Richmond MMM.
[16] NYCRO, R/Q/R 1/125, Richmond MMM.
[17] NYCRO, R/Q/R 5/311 & 10/224, minor alterations, 1896. Dobinson Trust Accounts, loc. cit.
[18] John W. Braithwaite: *Kirkby Stephen Almanac and Directory*, 1906.
[19] Reported to London Yearly Meeting, 1932.
[20] *The Friend*, Vol. 91, 1933, p. 577; *The Dalesman*, Vol. 21, June 1959, p. 207.

Countersett Friends Meeting House   (pages 64-69)
[1] NYCRO, R/Q/R 10/177, Account, 1732.

² Thomas Crosfield (ed.): *Memoirs of the Life and Gospel Labours of Samuel Fothergill*, 1843, p. 358. B. C. Corner and C. C. Booth: *Chain of Friendship. Selected Letters of Dr. John Fothergill*, 1971, O.U.P., p. 229.
³ John Woolman: *The Journal of*, 1900, p. 241. Henry J. Cadbury: *John Woolman in England, 1772*, 1971, pp. 82-136.
⁴ NYCRO, R/Q/R 1/186, Wensleydale, PMM.
⁵ NYCRO, R/Q/R 2/4/13-14, Conveyance, 18 & 19 January, 1778.
⁶ Ibid.
⁷ NYCRO, R/Q/R 1/187, Wensleydale PMM.
⁸ NYCRO, R/Q/R 1/121, Richmond MMM.
⁹ Ibid.
¹⁰ NYCRO, R/Q/R 1/189, Wensleydale PMM.
¹¹ NYCRO, R/Q/R 1/121-122, Richmond MMM.
¹² William Howitt: *The Rural Life in England*, 1838, pp. 299-300.
¹³ Jessie Fothergill: *Kith and Kin*, 1881 (1899 reprint, pp. 193-98).
¹⁴ Dobinson Trust Account Book, 1858-1932, consulted at Carperby Meeting House, c.1974.
¹⁵ Middleham Primitive Methodist Circuit Plan, 1872, consulted at Askrigg Moor Road Chapel, c.1964. FHLL, MS. Vol. 176, 'Narrative of the Friends Mission in Hawes and Wensleydale' by Norman Penney, 1882-86.
¹⁶ Harry Holroyd (ed.): *Methodism in Wensleydale 1765-1965*, Leyburn, 1965, pp. 23-4.
¹⁷ NYCRO, R/Q/R 1/125, Richmond MMM.
¹⁸ Hiscock's *Wensleydale and Swaledale Almanac*, Hawes, 1903, n.p.
¹⁹ Borthwick Institute, York, MRD 2/1/2-7, Annual Trust Property Schedules.

Countersett Friends School *(pages 69-72)*

¹ J. Stonestreet and D. Hall: *Raydaleside*, Askrigg, 1969, pp. 22-24.
² B. C. Corner and C. C. Booth: *Chain of Friendship. Selected Letters of Dr. John Fothergill*, 1971, O.U.P., p. 208.
³ LCLA, Richard Robinson's will, 1765, John Robinson's will, 1777.
⁴ NYCRO, R/Q/R 1/187, Wensleydale, PMM.
⁵ Ibid.
⁶ Jessie Fothergill: *Kith and Kin*, 1881 (1899 reprint, p. 96).
⁷ NYCRO, PR/STB, Stalling Busk Marriage register. Anna Jean Heard: *Journey into the Past*, Islington, Ontario, Canada, 1968.
⁸ NYCRO, R/Q/R 1/121, Richmond MMM.
⁹ Bernard Thistlethwaite: *The Thistlethwaite Family*, 1910, pp. 23-24.
¹⁰ William White: *History, Gazetteer and Directory of the East and North Ridings of Yorkshire*, Leeds, 1840, 606-10.
¹¹ Mr. Leslie Baily of Saffron Walden, pers. comm., 9 March & 9 October, 1971.
¹² PRO, HO 107/2380, Census 1851.
¹³ Recalled by the late Christopher Metcalfe, Burtersett, c.1974.
¹⁴ PRO, RG 9/3671, Census 1861.
¹⁵ Recalled by the late John M. Outhwaite, Skipton, c.1969.
¹⁶ Dobinson Trust Account Book, 1858-1932, consulted at Carperby Meeting House, c.1974.
¹⁷ NYCRO, R/Q/R 2/4/61, Agreement, 6 April, 1869.
¹⁸ PRO, RG 10/4870, Census 1871.

[19] Edward Kelly: *The Post Office Directory of the North and East Ridings of Yorkshire,* 1872, p. 93.
[20] Dobinson Trust Accounts, loc. cit. Recalled by the late Mrs. Mary I. Kettlewell, Askrigg, and John M. Outhwaite, Skipton, c.1965.
[21] NYCRO, R/Q/R 1/124, Richmond MMM.
[22] Ibid.
[23] Dobinson Trust Accounts, loc. cit. NYCRO, R/Q/R 1/124, Richmond MMM.
[24] Recollections of Miss Annie Dinsdale of Bainbridge, recalled by the late Mrs. Edna Outhwaite, Carr End, c.1960.
[25] Dobinson Trust Accounts, loc. cit.

Index

ACKWORTH School, 71
Adult School, 62-3
Agriculture: stock and husbandry, 4, 6, 24-5, 27-8, 32, 46-50, 55, 61
Airey (Aira, Array): John, 19, 58; William, 55
America, 14, 40, 66
Appersett, 44, 63
Askrigg, xiv, xv, 2-3, 8, 32, 40, 47, 50, 53-6
Atkinson: George, 8; Isabel, 9; John, 8; Richard, 9-10; Thomas, 8
Audland, John, 2
Australia, 40-1
Aysgarth, xv, 18, 22, 32, 47, 63

BAIN, river, xii, 44
Bainbridge: xiv, 9, 22, 25, 47, 55-6, 59, 61; Calffy yate, 60, 71; Holme Bray, 9, 19, 58-60; Manor, 4-5, 8, 20, 29-30, 35; Meeting House and Burial Ground, xii, 4, 9, 14, 18-9, 22, 24-5, 29, 31-3, 40, 42, 48, 58-61, 63, 66-7; Pasture Meeting, 9-10; Temperance Hall, 58-9
Baines, John, 50
Band of Hope, 59
Barker, Robert, 15
Barnard Castle, xv
Beckwith, Marmaduke, 11
Bedale, xv
Beedon, Thomas, 9
Bees, 6
Bell: Ann, 52, 54; Mary, 53-4; Matthew, 52-4; Paul, 53; Richard, 52; William, 52, 54
Benson, Gervase, xv
Bentley: Elizabeth *see* Robinson; Greenwood, 39
Beresford, Peter, 56
Besson, Richard, 7
Binks: Elizabeth, 9; John, 19; Richard, 9, 19
Birk Rigg, 4, 18
Bishop Auckland, xv
Bishopdale, 11

Blackburn, 39-40, 47, 52
Blades (Blaydes): Bartholomew, 7-8; Edmond, 7-8; James, 25
Blakey: Anne, 70; Elizabeth *see* Robinson; John, 38, 53; Joshua, 35, 38, 53, 67; Joshua Robinson, 53; Robert, 67, 70-1; Thomas, 66, 70; William, 26, 30-1, 33
Blaykling: John, xiv; Mary, xvi
Blean, 44, 46, 55, 71
Blenkiron, Thompson, 54
Boar (Board) Inn, 30, 42, 45, 47, 54-7, 71
Bolton Hall (New Bolton), 15
Borratt, xv
Bousfield, Major Miles, xv
Bowland, xiv
Bowling near Bradford, 36, 38, 53
Bradford, xvii, 36-9, 49-50, 79
Bridges: Isles, 32; Semerwater, 32-5
Brigflatts, xv, xvi, 66
Brighouse Monthly Meeting, 39
Broughill near Bainbridge, 9, 58
Brunskill: Alice, 56; Jane, 71; Simon, 56; Thomas, 56
Burtersett, 20, 22, 26, 44
Burton, Richard, 53

CALVERLEY Lodge near Bradford, 39
Calvert: James, 19, 25; Thomas, 10
Cam Fell, 22
Canada, 54, 70
Carlton in Coverdale, 11, 18
Carperby, xv, 2, 18, 31, 63
Carr End, xvi, 10, 14, 18, 25, 30, 36, 38, 42, 46, 53, 57, 66, 68-9
Carter, Richard, 71
Cartographers, 45, 48, 51, 56
Castle Bolton, 1
Cautley in Cumbria, xv
Charity (Quaker), 10, 14, 25, 28, 31, 55
Chaytor, John, 10, 16-7, 21
Church rate, xv, 8, 11, 46
Clapham, Christopher, 6
Clarendon Code, 6

85

Coates: Ann, 49; Anne, 70; Elizabeth, 54; James, 49, 54; John, 53; Joseph, 54; Mary, 54; Rose Hannah, 54; Thomas, 53-4
Cockfighting, xv
Commons: Bainbridgeside, 6, 25, 29, 35, 49; Bardale, 6, 25, 29, 49, 56; Countersett Crag, 6, 22, 25, 27, 29, 35, 42, 49
Congregationalists, 59
Constables, 6-8
Coopermire, 39, 42, 47-8, 56-7
Coultherd, Edmund, 56
Countersett: xii, xvii, 2-4, 6-7, 10, 13, 25-6, 28-9, 33, 40, 42, 44, 48, Hall, xii, xviii, 1-5, 11, 13-4, 18-20, 22, 26-7, 29-30, 32, 35-6, 39, 42-8, 54-7, 64, 72; Meeting House, xii, 22-6, 30, 35-8, 42, 50, 56, 59, 64-9, 71-2; School, xii, 33, 35-6, 42, 69, 72
Coverdale, xiv, xv, 11-3
Coward, Ann, 9, 58
Craddock: Joseph, 11, 13; Thomas, 13, 76
Crawshawbooth, 46
Cupplesfield, 44

Dale Grange, 50
Darlington, xv
Dent, Ann, 53
Dentdale, xv, 63
Dialect, 6, 14, 75-6
Dinsdale, Annie, 84
Distrainment, xv, 7-9, 32, 46
Dobinson, Joseph, 25, 28, 53, 59-60
Dodd Fell, 22
Dower: Arthur, 47-8, 56; Jean, 47-8, 56
Drawell, xvi, 10
Drovers, 8

Easby, xv
Easingwold, xv
Ecclesfield, 70
Eccleshill Hall near Bradford, 39
Edgar, Eleanor, 49
Edinburgh, 53
Elliott, Margaret, 79
Emigration, 14, 40-1, 54, 70

Farnsworth, Richard, xiv
Fawcett: Thomas, 9, 54, 61; John, 56
Fell, Leonard, 11
Fieldgate near Bainbridge, 71
Fieldnames, 10, 24, 26-30, 35, 37-9, 44-5, 47-9, 53, 55, 57, 60
Fifth Monarchy Rising, 6, 8

Firbank Fell, xv
Flora, 67, 69-70
Flugel, S.M.I., 47
Fothergill: Anthony, 30; Alexander, d 1695, 10, 19; Alexander, d 1788, 28, 31, 33-6, 56, 59, 66, 69; Alexander, d 1843, 70; Hannah see Robinson; Jessie, 68-70; John, d 1684, 11, 18; John, d 1744, xvi, 25, 31-2, 56; Dr. John, 36, 66, 69; John, d 1858, 38; Samuel, 31, 66; William, 36
Fox: George, xiv-xvi, 1-2, 6, 8, 10-1, 13, 18, 46, 64, 67; Journal, xiv-xv, 10-1; Margaret, 10-1
Friends Mission, 63, 68

Garsdale, xv, 11
Geldart, Richard, 11-2
Gibson: Elizabeth see Robinson; George, 36; Thomas, 9
Gill Edge near Bainbridge, 44, 48
Gilling, xv
Glover, Robert, 69
Gorton, James, 22
Gosling, Robert, 10
Goole, 39
Grainger, Mary, 71
Grayrigg, 2
Greenscarmire, 56
Greenwood, C., Cartographer, 56
Gregson, Jane, 54
Grindleton, xiv
Grinton, xv, 14, 54
Grizedale, xv
Gunter, John, 21
Gurnell: James, 7, 10; Jane, 10

Haistwell, Edward, 11
Hall: Ernest, 47; Margaret, 47
Harecoursing, 22
Hartforth (Hartford), 15, 21
Harrison: Alice, 33; Bartholomew, 7, 9-10, 14, 44, 54-6; Daniel, 33, 46; Edmond, 4, 58; Edward, 9-10, 14, 22; Elizabeth, 33, 53; Hannah, 55; Isabell, 7, 10, 54-5; Margaret, 33, 55; John, 10; Reuben, 30, 33, 46, 49, 55
Hawes: xiv, 11, 59, 61; Adult School, 62-3; Friends Mission, 69; Meeting House and Burial Ground, xii, xv, 14, 18, 25, 31, 42, 58, 61-4, 69
Healaugh Park, Swaledale, xvi
Hearth Tax, 5, 14, 58, 76
High Forse, Raydaleside, 46
High Burton, xvi, 11

Hillary: Isaac, 27, 29; John, 4, 18-20, 24-6, 29; Margaret, 24; Mary *see* Robinson; Dr. William, 36
Hills, Richard, 4
Hird, Thomas, 8
Hodgson: Abraham, 25; John, 56; Jinny, 56
Holly (Holling) House, 4, 20, 24-5, 30-1, 35, 38-40, 42, 44, 47-9, 52-4, 70
Holme Bray, Bainbridge, 9, 19, 58-60
Horse Racing, xv
Horse Silver, 28
Horton Gill (Raygill), 22
Hosier, 6
Household Goods, 7-8, 24, 28, 32, 35, 38
Howgill: xv; Francis, 2
Howitt, William, 46, 67
Hoyle, Elizabeth *see* Robinson
Hubberthorne, Richard, 2, 64
Hudswell, xv
Hunter: Agnes, 37, 50; Margaret, 71
Hutton, 2

IANSON, James, 22
Informers, 8-9
Inns, xiv, 30, 42, 45, 47, 54-7, 71
Isles Bridge near Low Row in Swaledale, 32

JACKSON, Henry, 6; Sidney, 79
Jamaica, 4, 10
Jeffery, Thomas, Cartographer, 48, 56
Johnson, Thomas, 10, 17

KEARTON in Swaledale, xvi
Kellet, 11
Kettlewell: 15; Mary, I., 84
Kilburn: Elizabeth, 47, 54; Matthew, 47, 54
Kingston upon Hull, 39
Kirkbride: Elsie, 56; Fred, 56
Kirkby Lonsdale, xv
Kirkby Stephen, xv
Knaresborough Monthly Meeting, 31
Knitting: 72; Hosier, 55

LAMBERT: Ann, 53; Isabel, 9; John, 9; Mary, 8-9; Thomas, 25, 34-5, 53, 67
Lancaster, John, 4
Land Tax, 32
Langstrothdale, xv, 11, 46
Lay Subsidy, 42
Lead Mining, xv, 15-6, 21-2
Lea Yeat, Kirby Malham, 26
Lea Yet, Dentdale, 63, 71

Le Patourel, H. E. J., 79
Leyburn, 18, 22
Littondale, 11
London, xv, xvi, 2, 4, 5, 8, 31
London Morning Meeting, 31
Lonsdale, Jeffrey, 66
Low Ellington, xvi
Low Foss, Raydaleside, 50
Low or Chapel House Farm, Countersett, 23, 30, 56

MALLERSTANG, xv
Malhamdale, xiv
Marsett, xii, 44, 47, 53-4, 56, 68, 71
Marsden Meeting House, 30, 46, 53
Marrick, xv
Marske, xv, 54
Masham, xvi, 11-3, 16
Mason: George, xv; Thomas, xv; William, 9, 14, 58
Masons Arms, Raydaleside, 55
Mastiles Lane, xiv
Medicine, xvii, 36, 38-40, 50, 70
Medieval Pottery, 47
Metcalfe: Ann, 9; Ann *see* Robinson; Alexander, 4, 10, 19; Anthony, 10, 19; Augustine, 10; Christopher, 71, 83; Ellen, 56; Elizabeth, 53; Francis, 9, 19, 33; George, 24, 25, 28; James, 6, 8, 13, 19, 24-5, 27-8, 56, 68; John, 4, 33, 56; Margaret, 10; Mary, 63; Reuben, 33, 35; Richard, 53; Thomas, 25, 31, 49, 55; William, 19, 56
Methodist (*see* also Primitive), 53-4, 69
Middleham, xiv, xv, 3, 11
Middlemas (Middlemiss): Elizabeth, 40; Elsie, 43; Thomas, 40; Walter, 56
Milnthorpe, 10
Mires, Christopher, 56
Missions (Quaker), 63, 68
Morland, John, 17
Monkhouse, W., Cartographer, 45, 51
Mount Pleasant near Bradford, 39
Mudd, James, 71-2

NEWCASTLE, 2
New Close House, 30, 55
New Inn, Raydaleside, 55
Nichols, Samuel, 46, 49
Nicholson: Christopher, 25; Stephen, 59; Thomas, 9, 59
North Riding County Council, 64; Quarter Sessions, 7, 8, 18, 22, 25, 34, 55, 58
Nottingham, xv

87

OCCUPATIONS, 1, 4, 8, 15, 17, 38-41, 46-7, 52-3, 55, 60, 63, 71
Ogden, John, 25
Orton, William, 15
Outhett, John, 34
Outhwaite: Edna, 84; John, 71; John, M., 83-4

PALEY: Dorothy, 54; Ellen, 47; Francis, 47, 54; George, 46; Hannah, 47, 56; John, 46, 72; Joseph, 47, 54; Mary, 46-7; Thomas, 47
Park Rash, xiv
Peacock: Brian, 48; Christopher, 48; Margaret, 48
Pease, John, M.P., 67
Pendle Hill, xiv
Penketh School, 71
Penney, Norman, 62-3, 68
Pilkington: James, M.P., 52; William, 39-40, 47, 52-3
Poolbank, Cumbria, 10
Potts, John, 19, 25
Pratt: Hannah, 19, 48, 53; Jane *see* Robinson; Joseph, 48, 53; Mary, xvi, 33; Michael, 9, 58
Preston: Dorothy, 54; George, 40, 54
Preston Patrick, xv, 2
Preston under Scarr, 1
Primitive Methodist, 65, 68
Proctor, Eleanor, 30

QUAKERS *see* Religious Society of Friends

RAISGILL, 56
Ravenstonedale, xv
Raydale (Radall), 44
Raydaleside, xii, xiii, xvii, 4, 14, 22, 33, 35, 38, 44, 48, 52, 55, 59, 69, 71
Redmire, 1, 32
Reed, Elizabeth of Jamaica, 10
Religious Society of Friends, xii, xv, xvii, 2-3, 6, 10, 20
Ribblesdale, xiv
Richardson: Elizabeth, 19; John, 19; William, 19
Richmond: xiv, xv, 2-3, 5-9, 12-3, 63; Consistory Court, 8, 10-1; House of Correction, 7-8, 11-2, 16; Monthly Meeting, xv, xvi, xvii, 28, 31, 38, 50, 63, 67, 70, 72; Preparative Meeting, xvi
Rigoll, Margaret, 41, 79
Roberts: Margaret *see* Robinson; Sharp, 38

Robinson, Abel, 1710-31, 26
Amos, 1697-1775, xvi, xvii, 25-7, 29-38, 46, 48, 53, 55, 61
Amos, 1835-, 39-41
Ann (*née* Metcalfe), c. 1700-30, *m* 1729, Amos Robinson, 29, 48   Ann
Elizabeth, *m* John Robinson, 40,
51
Benjamin, 1698-1784, 26, 28, 30, 33, 36
Charlotte, 1816-, *m* 1853, John Wood, 39
Christopher, -1653, 1
Edward, 1665-, 4
Elizabeth (*née* Smith), 1664-1742, *m* 1689, John Robinson, 19, 25, 28-9
Elizabeth, 1706-40, *m* 1733, William Blakey, 26
Elizabeth (*née* Hoyle), 1729-1804, *m* 1754, Joshua Robinson, *m* 1778, George Gibson from Saffron Walden, 30, 35-6, 38, 53
Elizabeth (*née* Walker), 1744-1810, *m* 1744, John Robinson, 37-8
Elizabeth, 1749-49, 31
Elizabeth, Isabella, 1782-1808, 38
Elizabeth, 1812-, *m* Greenwood Bentley, 39
Emanuel, 1668-, 4, 24
Ephraim, 1662-1735, 4, 19-20, 24-5, 29, 53, 59
George, 1655-75, 4, 10
Hannah, 1733-1836, *m* 1782, William Fothergill, 31, 33, 36-7, 46
Helen, 1815-, 39
Henry Semerdale, 1855-, 41
Henry Wood, 1829-99, 39-41
Jane (*née* Pratt), 1713-94, *m* 1747, Amos Robinson, 31, 35-7, 46, 48, 53
Jane, c. 1790-, *m* Alexander Fothergill, xiii
Jane Beatrix, 1780-, *m* 1804, Thomas Saunderson, 38
Jeffrey Wood, 1831-, 39-41
John, 1658-1739, xvi, 4, 18-20, 22, 24-30, 38, 44, 46, 48, 53, 55-6, 59
John, 1700-77, 26, 29, 30, 32-5, 46, 56, 60, 69
John, 1750-1811, xvii, 10, 31, 33, 35-8, 48-9, 53, 66, 69
John, 1778-1853, 38-9, 49-50, 56
John, 1821-, 39-41, 50-1, 54
Joshua, 1712-75, 26, 29-35, 53
Joshua Walker, 1810-, 39
Margaret, c. 1630-89, *m* Richard Robinson, 4, 10, 18, 20, 25, 43-4

Robinson—*cont.*
Margaret, 1690-, 26
Margaret, 1775-, *m* Sharp Roberts, 37-8, 48
Margaret (*née* Wood), 1793-1853, 39, 50, 52
Mary, 1661-1733, *m* 1692, John Hillary, 4, 18-9, 27, 29
Mary, c.1780-c.1817, *m* John Robinson, 38-9, 49-50, 53
Mary, 1813-, 39
Michael, 1593-, 1
Michael, 1653-1712, 4, 10, 13-4, 17, 19-22, 24-5, 27, 29, 38, 44, 53, 58, 64, 66
Rachel, 1673-1759, 4, 17, 19, 24, 28
Rebecca, 1672-72, 4
Richard of Countersett: Ancestry and Parentage, xvii, 1; Early Life and Education, xvii, 1, 2; Marriage, xvii, 4; To Countersett, xii, 4, 5; Siblings, 4, 10, 19-20, 25; Status, vii, 4-6, 17, 43-4; and Law, xv, 2, 4, 5, 8-9, 16-7, 22; Lead Mining, xv, 15-6; Bainbridge Manor, 4-5, 8; Convinced, xv, 1-2; Moral and Physical Characteristics, xvi, 1-3, 10, 18, 19; Quaker Missionary, xii, xv, 2, 5, 16, 19; Valiant Sixty, 18; Contact with George Fox, xiv, xv, 2, 10-1, 13, 18; Confusion re his name, xvi; Going Naked, 3; Suffering for Truth, xv, 2-3, 6, 8-10; Distrained upon, 6-7; Recorder of Sufferings, xv, 9, 12, 14, 55; A Prisoner, xv, 6-8, 11-3, 16; Works, *A Warning to the Inhabitants of the Whole Earth,* 1679; *A Blast Blown out of the North and Ecchoing up towards the South, to meet the Cry of their Oppressed Brethren,* 1680, xv, 9, 12-3, 18; Manuscripts, ii, xv, 14-5; Death, Burial and Testimonies, 19, 61
Richard of Brigflatts, xv, xvi
Richard of Healaugh Park, xv, xvi
Richard of High Burton, xv, xvi
Richard of Roecliffe, xv, xvi
Richard, 1694-1765, 25-6, 28-30, 32-3, 35, 38, 46, 53, 55-6, 59-60, 66, 69
Richard, 1751-52, 31
Richard, 1776-85, 37
Richard, 1824-67, 39-41
Richard Amos, 1868-, 41
Susannah, 1692-1772, 26, 28, 30, 33
Symon, 1

Robinsons' Reef Gold Mine, 41
Routh (Rowth): Alice, 9; Christopher, 9-11, 13, 19; Elizabeth, 9, 19, 50, 58; John, 19; Lawrence, 14; Mary, 71; Oswold, 9, 19, 61-2; Richard, 7, 9, 19, 71; Seth, 9; Thomas, 9, 19; William, 71
Ripon, xv
Roecliffe, xvi
Ross: Florence, 54; Malcolm, 54
Rossal, Rose Hannah, 54
Rowntree, Fred, Architect, 60
Rudd, Thomas, 16

SANDEMANIANS, 63
Saunderson: Jane Beatrix *see* Robinson; Thomas, 38
Sawley, xiv
Scarrhouse in Langstrothdale, xv, 11
Schools, xii, 33, 35-6, 42, 60, 69-72, 84
Scott: Edward, 25; James, 25; John, 72; Joseph, 58
Sedbergh, xiv, xv, 2, 10-1, 36
Seekers, xiv, 2
Semerdale Hall (House) and farm, 4, 17-8, 25-7, 29, 32, 35-42, 44, 48-54
Semerwater: xii, 28, 44, 46; Bridge, 32-5
Settle, xv
Shaw: Fanny, 72; Jonathan, 38, 48-9
Sibford School, 71
Sill, John, 49
Simson, Mary, 19
Skipton, 11
Smith: Ann 33; Dorothy, 54; Elizabeth *see* Robinson; Hannah, 55
Smithson, Francis, 4, 15, 31
Snowdon, John, 2
Spence, Mary, 9
Stake Road, 11
Stalling Busk, xii, 44, 49-50, 53-7, 69, 72
Stockdale (Stockdall): Alexander, 19; James, 22; John, 9, 19, 58; Jonas, 9
Stockton, xv, 16
Sufferings (Quaker), xv, 6-9, 11-4, 18, 32, 46, 54
Sundial House, Bradford, 36
Swarthmore, 10
Swale, Philip, xv, 10, 13, 15-7, 21, 28, 76
Swaledale, xvi, 2, 9, 12-4, 21
Swineley in Widdale, 63, 71
Swinithwaite, 32, 52

TAYLOR: James, 4; Richard, 61; Thomas, 2, 13
Temperance, 58-60
Tennant: John, xiv, 46, 55; Stephen 10

Terry, Richard, 66
Thirsk, xv, 8, 18
Thistlethwaite: Agnes, 37, 50; Elizabeth, 46; James, 71; John, 50, 70; Margaret, 71; Richard, 37, 50, 71; William, 71
Thompson: Francis, 9-10, 19; Jacob, 10; James, 9, 19, 25; John, 9-10; Margaret, 55; Thomas, 14-5, 25
Thornaby, William, 9, 13
Thornborrow: George, 56; Vera, 56
Thornesfield House near Wakefield, 40, 52
Thorns House, Raydaleside, 30, 53
Thornton Rust, 55
Thwaite (Thwaytes): Ann, 33; Anthony, 4, 24; James, 24, 33; John, 34-5; Simon, 30
Tithe, xv, 6, 18, 32, 46, 54
Todd: Christopher, 7; Dorothy, 9, 58
Todthorne, near Grayrigg, 2
Toleration Act, 18
Tomlin, Ann, 49
Tomlinson, Robert, 33
Turnpike, Richmond and Lancaster, 56

UPPER House, Bowling, Bradford, 36-9

VACCARY, 42, 48
Valiant Sixty, xiv, 18
Verity House, Countersett, 30, 36, 42, 56
Verity: Margaret, 28; Richard, 56; Roger, 56
Vernacular Achitecture, 1, 4-5, 14, 26-7, 30-1, 35-6, 42-4, 49, 53, 55, 58-9

WADDINGTON, Margaret, 37-8
Walker: Elizabeth *see* Robinson; Joshua, 36-8; Margaret, 37-8
Weatherald (Wetherald, Wetheralt): James, 7, 19, 25, 54, 61; John, 35; Thomas, 63, 72

Webster: Ann, 56; Percy, 56; William, 71
Wensley, xv, 1
Wensleydale, xii, xiv, xv, 1-2, 5-6, 9, 11-3, 19
Wensleydale Preparative Meeting, xvi, 2, 6, 9-11, 13-4, 18-9, 22, 24, 33, 58-61, 63-4, 67
West: Pat, 48; Robin, 48
West Burton, 18
Westmorland, xiv, xv, 2, 10-1, 16, 21, 31
West Witton, 18, 32
Wether Fell, 22
Wharfedale, xiv
Wharton: Humphery, 13, 76; Philip, 14-5
White: Hannah, 47; James, 52; John, 50
Widdale, 71
Wilson, James, 31
Williamson, Isabel, 9
Wilkinson/Story Debate, 10
Wilmslow School, 71
Winn, Stephen, 11-2, 15
Winchester, Marquess of, 15
Wood End, Raydaleside, 56
Wood: Margaret *see* Robinson; James Burton, 39-40; John, 39; Rev. Richard, 52
Woolman, John, 66
Wyatt, Alfred, 68
Wynn, Cuthbert, 5

YARM, xv, 16
Yearly Meeting of the Religious Society of Friends, 64
Yore river, xii
Yorebridge School, xiv
York: xv, 2; Castle, 6-8
Yorkshire: xiv, xv, 11; Yorkshire Plot, The, 8